PERSPECTIVES

DATE DUE

Relevant Scenes for Teens

MARY KRELL-OISHI

MERIWETHER PUBLISHING LTD.
Colorado Springs, Colorado

Meriwether Publishing Ltd., Publisher
P.O. Box 7710
Colorado Springs, CO 80933

Executive editor: Theodore O. Zapel
Typesetting: Sharon E. Garlock and Sue Trinko
Cover design: Tom Myers

NOTICE FOR PROFESSIONAL PRODUCTION
For any form of non-amateur presentation (professional stage, radio or television), permission must be obtained in writing from the publisher, Meriwether Publishing Ltd. (address above).

Library of Congress Cataloging-in-Publication Data

Krell-Oishi, Mary, 1953-
    Perspectives : relevant scenes for teens / Mary Krell-Oishi.
        p.   cm.
    Summary: Consists of scenes in a variety of styles for high school and college acting students featuring scripts in five subject categories: dating, pregnancy, control, family, and growing up.
        ISBN 1-56608-030-4 (paper)
        1. Acting. 2. Young adult drama, American. 3. Teenagers--Drama.
    [1. Acting. 2. Plays. 3. Teenagers--Drama.] I. Title.
    PN2080.K74   1997
    812'.54--dc21   97-5405
                                                                        CIP
                                                                        AC

1   2   3   4   5   6   7   8   99   98   97

For my students at Sunny Hills who bring me such joy.
And, of course, for my family, who give me such love.

Contents

PREFACE

Organizing this collection of scenes was a challenge that I looked forward to undertaking. Because I am, above all, a high school theatre teacher, I wanted to write things that would be useful not only to my own program, but that could be easily adapted for use by other teachers. I mulled over what it was I looked for when choosing work for my advanced acting students. I came up with the following criteria: Challenging subject matter, characters with a degree of depth within their reach, variety of style and equal distribution between men and women. I believe I have achieved my goals with this book.

Within each section of *Perspectives,* there are several scenes, each running between ten and fifteen minutes. These sections lend themselves to a full-length performance or are easily played as separate scenes. Also, should you choose to set a "themed performance," you have the ability to double cast your actors in more than one scene. (And what a brave soul you would be!) The sections lend themselves to discussion formats, encouraging interaction between audience and actor after the performance guided by the instructor. My ideal choice would be a week of after-school performances with a question and answer format immediately following. However, the choices are up to you.

The sections deal with young adult Perspectives on the subjects of Dating, Family, Teen Pregnancy, Control, and Growing Up. While some of the scenes are humorous, especially in the Dating Perspective, many take a more serious look at the conditions presented. The language is a bit stronger, the subject matter, relevant to contemporary society, is sometimes difficult to take, but, then, so can life be. It is how problems are faced that ultimately creates character.

I hope that you find that these scenes suit your needs as a teacher and that your young actors find the depth within the characters.

Again, let me thank my students at Sunny Hills High School. They act as my guinea pigs, my cheering section, and allow me as an observer into their lives. All teachers should be as fortunate as I have been to work with such talented and generous young people. Enjoy and create.

Mary Krell-Oishi
May 1996

FOREWORD

What Mary Krell-Oishi has created in *Perspectives* is a gold mine of theatrical literature for high school/college-age actors. She mixes humor with pathos to create the world of the teenager in scenes and monologs. Mrs. Krell-Oishi writes of her own youth experiences and those she observes of her students, blending situations involving friends and family into a dramatic form, suitable for classroom scene study and/or performance.

These scenes provide opportunities for young actors to play roles that address friendship, divorce, commitment, the empowerment of females, youthful love, the feelings of being a loser and a success. Some of the material deals with serious issues; some with lighthearted looks at everyday life. The playwright presents a teen perspective that relates to the fourteen-year-old to the nineteen-year-old; the freshman in high school to the freshman in college; to any sensitive young actor who deals in real-life situations. These scenes work well individually or combined into an evening of performance. They can be used as audition pieces, classroom scenes, festival entries and discussion ignitors.

I truly believe that Mary Krell-Oishi sees life as her character, Charlie, does in "Where You Going?" when he says:

> You know, you never really get a chance to appreciate the beauty of a parking lot until it's empty. The symmetry of the lines marking each stall. The contrast of the white paint against the black of the asphalt. It really is a beautiful thing.

Those of us who work with teenagers in Educational Theatre settings want to guide them to understand their lives and the changing world around them. As Mrs. Krell-Oishi states... "It really is a beautiful thing."

I feel proud to know Mary as a friend, colleague, contemporary, playwright, and fellow board member. I love to judge at International Festivals and hear the young actors state the name of the playwright as my friend, Mary Krell-Oishi.

I thank Mary Krell-Oishi for writing material that challenges young actors' skills, imaginations, moral values and emotions.

Gai Jones
Educational Theatre Director
Region I Director of Educational Theatre Association

1

Perspectives on
DATING

Blowkiss

(Scene for one man and one woman)

1   *(JON and JEN: It is important for these characters to be*
2   *played as good friends. There should be no hint of any kind*
3   *of romantic or "sexual tension" stuff between them. They*
4   *are, above all, compatriots. The scene takes place at JEN's*
5   *home.)*
6   **JON:** Jen, are you here?
7   **JEN:** I'm in the bathroom, just a second.
8   **JON:** Take your time. I don't have anywhere to go.
9   **JEN:** I thought you had a date.
10 **JON:** Nah. Didn't work out.
11 **JEN:** How come?
12 **JON:** We just didn't, I don't know...sync.
13 **JEN:** *(Entering in robe, drying hair)* Sync?
14 **JON:** Sync. You know, blend, meld, form as one, come together.
15 **JEN:** Oh. Sync.
16 **JON:** *(Picking up apple)* You gonna eat this?
17 **JEN:** No.
18 **JON:** *(Taking a bite)* Yum. Tart.
19 **JEN:** Yeah?
20 **JON:** Yeah. Tart, but not too tart. *(Taking another bite)* Kind of
21   sweet, too.
22 **JEN:** So, it's a good apple?
23 **JON:** As apples go, yes, I would say that this is a good apple. A
24   very good apple. This is a top-of-the-line apple.
25 **JEN:** Good. *(She begins combing out her hair.)*
26 **JON:** You've got great hair.
27 **JEN:** But would you call it top-of-the-line hair?
28 **JON:** Hmmm. Top-of-the-line hair, you say? Let me see. Yes, I
29   would definitely call this hair top-of-the-line hair. Thick.
30   Black, almost pitch in color. *(He sniffs her hair.)* Fragrant.
31   Yes, top-of-the-line hair. Top-of-the-line apple, top-of-the-
32   line hair.
33 **JEN:** Having a good day, are you?
34 **JON:** A good day. Not a top-of-the-line day, but a good day all
35   in all.

1   JEN: So, what happened to your date?
2   JON: Didn't work out. We didn't...
3   JEN: Sync...
4   JON: Sync...yes.
5   JEN: What does that mean, exactly?
6   JON: Well, OK. OK. For example, she's a blower.
7   JEN: A blower? I think I've heard enough.
8   JON: Don't be lewd. No, she's a blower. She blows a lot. Like
9   my ear, my neck, she even blew on my eyes.
10 JEN: Some people might find that sexy.
11 JON: Not if they wear contact lenses.
12 JEN: I see the problem. OK, she blew on you. That's not so
13   bad. She can be retrained.
14 JON: No...she's too far gone. Beyond all hope. She's a
15   blowkisser.
16 JEN: No!
17 JON: I swear to you!
18 JEN: No!
19 JON: *(Pointing to his mouth)* Right here. Right here. She blew
20   on me.
21 JEN: I've heard of that, but I have never experienced it.
22   Omigod. What was it like? I mean, details.
23 JON: You don't understand. It was the most bizarre thing.
24   Took me completely by surprise.
25 JEN: I can only imagine.
26 JON: No, you have no idea.
27 JEN: How did it happen? Did she just pounce on you?
28 JON: That was the strangest part. There we were. You know
29   how it is after a first date. You're driving home,
30   wondering should I? Shouldn't I?
31 JEN: That is the worst. I hate that part of the first date.
32 JON: A nightmare.
33 JEN: Go on, so what happened? You're driving home.
34 JON: Well, I thought things were going pretty well. She
35   laughed at my jokes, even the lame ones.

1   JEN: That's always a good sign.
2   JON: I think so. Not forced laughs, mind you, but true laughs.
3   Chuckles. I mean, she was a sincere laugher.
4   JEN: That's a good thing. I can see why you felt good.
5   JON: Oh, there's more. While we were at the movies...
6   JEN: What did you see?
7   JON: *Pulp Fiction.*
8   JEN: Again? Not a great date movie.
9   JON: It was a test. If she could like that movie, she was a girl I
10   could like.
11 JEN: And did she?
12 JON: That was the amazing thing. She loved it.
13 JEN: Well, there you go.
14 JON: I know. Who would have thought? So, anyway, there we
15   were, watching the movie and holding hands...
16 JEN: On the first date. That's so intimate...
17 JON: That's what I thought. But she seemed to want to, and
18   who am I to argue...?
19 JEN: Hand holding...
20 JON: I know, but that's how it was going...
21 JEN: The holding of hands...
22 JON: So, then, there we were, for the longest time.
23 JEN: Holding...
24 JON: Yes. And you know how your hand gets sweaty...
25 JEN: I hate that.
26 JON: But there's nothing you can do about it...
27 JEN: You are so right...
28 JON: Except to just release and wipe.
29 JEN: Yeah. I know, yes. Release and wipe. It has to be done...
30 JON: But, if you do it right, it's a sly move.
31 JEN: You think?
32 JON: Oh yeah, very smooth. You do the release and wipe, and
33   then, instead of going back to the everyday hand hold,
34   what you do is put your hand on top of hers, see? My
35   hand goes on top and then our fingers entwine.

1   JEN: Oh, that's good. I've never tried that. Fingers laced. I'll
2   have to remember that!
3   JON: The best thing about it is that way you still have hand
4   contact, but you allow yourself freedom of movement.
5   *(He demonstrates.)*
6   JEN: Sounds like everything was going so well.
7   JON: It was, it was. It gets better, too. What do you want me to
8   do with this apple?
9   JEN: You're done with it?
10 JON: Yeah.
11 JEN: You only ate half of it.
12 JON: I wasn't as hungry as I thought.
13 JEN: Then why did you start it?
14 JON: It looked good.
15 JEN: Huh, jeez, I hate when you do that. Just toss it in the
16   trash.
17 JON: You won't get ants?
18 JEN: I don't know. It's too cold for ants.
19 JON: I'll just hold it.
20 JEN: You're going to save it for later?
21 JON: Maybe.
22 JEN: Won't it turn brown?
23 JON: Not if I put lemon on it. Do you have any lemon?
24 JEN: I'll check. So, go on. How did it get better?
25 JON: On the drive home.
26 JEN: I hate that. I hate the drive home on a first date. Don't
27   you hate that?
28 JON: You don't even know. Torture.
29 JEN: It's worse for the woman. You are wondering if he will or
30   won't, and if he doesn't is it because your breath is bad,
31   and if you do, will he think you're easy. So many things to
32   think about. Your entire future is tied up in just those
33   few moments in the car on the way home from a movie.
34 JON: No, for the guy, you are wondering if you're going to get
35   turned down or what.

1   JEN: Stop. Girls don't turn guys down for a goodnight kiss.
2   Have you ever been?
3   JON: Let me think. No, I don't think I have.
4   JEN: We just don't. Even guys we have no intention of seeing
5   again we will at least toss them the P.K.
6   JON: P.K.?
7   JEN: Pity Kiss. I'll bet you've been P.K.'d and not even known
8   it.
9   JON: You think?
10 JEN: Oh, yeah. We do it all the time. Better to P.K. and get out
11   of the situation fast than to make excuses for hours on
12   end. I'm telling you, it's usually a P.K. and run.
13 JON: P.K. I'll have to remember that. P.K. OK, we're driving
14   home, and here comes the real test. The Chapstick Lip
15   Balm test.
16 JEN: No! You didn't.
17 JON: Not me...her!
18 JEN: Oh, she wanted you, she wanted you bad.
19 JON: I know. I know she did.
20 JEN: Strawberry?
21 JON: *(Meaningful pause)* Mango!
22 JEN: You are not serious.
23 JON: Why would I lie?
24 JEN: Mango...
25 JON: Mango. So, she puts it on. Puts it on and looks at me and
26   asks me...
27 JEN: Did you want to use it...
28 JON: That's right. So, I thought, make a decision. This was
29   obviously an invitation.
30 JEN: Of course it was. Her Chapstick, your lips. She was
31   telling you what she wanted.
32 JON: Those were my thoughts exactly.
33 JEN: So, you put it on...
34 JON: Yes, and I put it on good, too. I wanted to be ready for
35   anything.

1   JEN: Good thinking.

2   JON: I was a Boy Scout.

3   JEN: Be prepared.

4   JON: I was, I was prepared. But not for this. So we drive up
5   her driveway. Now, I was debating, do I get out and walk
6   her to the door, or sit in the car and just mac?

7   JEN: Mac? You just met the girl, this is the first date.

8   JON: We had shared the Chapstick.

9   JEN: Mango.

10   JON: Mango. But then I thought, no I am a gentleman and I
11   don't want her to be uncomfortable. So, I thought, no, I
12   will just walk her to her door. Hey, I'm a polite guy.

13   JEN: Yes you are.

14   JON: So, I take off my seat belt and look at her and then *bam!*
15   There she is.

16   JEN: I don't see how this could not work out. This was meant
17   to be. She was there...

18   JON: Right there. We were separated by mere molecules.

19   JEN: So, what happened?

20   JON: It started off OK. A little different, but exciting. You
21   know, because it was new.

22   JEN: The blowing?

23   JON: The blowing. See, first she would, like, kiss my cheek
24   and then she'd blow on it.

25   JEN: I don't get it.

26   JON: I didn't either. It was like... *(He demonstrates by kissing*
27   *the air and then blowing immediately after)* ...like that.

28   JEN: That is so weird.

29   JON: Isn't it? Let me show you. *(He leans over, blowkisses her*
30   *cheek.)*

31   JEN: Ewww. That is not sexy.

32   JON: I didn't think so, but hey, I'm for new things. So, there
33   she is blowkissing my face and my neck.

34   JEN: You found this exciting?

35   JON: I wouldn't say I found it exciting, no. I couldn't

1   concentrate. I started counting.
2 JEN: Counting what?
3 JON: The blowkisses. She got up to twenty-six before I finally
4   thought, OK, let's see what she does on the lips.
5 JEN: She blewkissed your face twenty-six times?
6 JON: I counted. I know for a fact it was twenty-six times.
7 JEN: And no lip contact yet?
8 JON: Nope. So I thought, kiss the girl and see what happens.
9   And I was *that* surprised when I felt my cheeks being
10   blown up like balloons.
11 JEN: No!
12 JON: I swear to you, like balloons.
13 JEN: What did you do?
14 JON: Well, she must have known that I was surprised. I just
15   sat back and looked at her, astounded...and blew the air
16   out of my mouth.
17 JEN: Was she embarrassed?
18 JON: *No!* Absolutely not. I even asked her. I said, "What was
19   that?" You know what she said?
20 JEN: Tell me...
21 JON: "Oh, it's what I do." Can you imagine?
22 JEN: "It's what I do?" That's like Jeffrey Dahmer saying "It's
23   what I do." How odd.
24 JON: Indeed, it was odd. So I thought, maybe that was just a
25   preliminary thing, so I leaned in to kiss her, you know,
26   the right way...
27 JEN: The way it's been done for centuries.
28 JON: Yes. So I kissed her, you know...
29 JEN: Yeah. And?
30 JON: From her reaction, I don't think she's ever been kissed
31   like that before.
32 JEN: No! Is she from this planet?
33 JON: Who knows. She asked me what I was doing, and I told
34   her, "It's what *I* do."
35 JEN: Good answer!

1   JON: It was, wasn't it? So, we just looked at each other and we
2   both knew we were not destined to mac that night or any
3   other night.
4   JEN: The blower versus the regular. It would never work.
5   JON: No. Never work. *(A reflection-filled pause)* You still going
6   to Mark's party?
7   JEN: Yeah. You wanna come? It should be fun.
8   JON: I have no plans. Yeah, why not.
9   JEN: Give me a minute to get dressed. *(She exits.)*
10 JON: Will there be food?
11 JEN: You didn't finish that apple and you want to be fed?
12 JON: I'm not in an apple mood. Will Tiffany be there?
13 JEN: She said she would.
14 JON: I need normal. No more blowing on my face or in my
15   mouth, not for this boy.
16
17
18
19
20
21
22
23
24
25
26
27
28
29
30
31
32
33
34
35

Pre-Party Plans

(Scene for four men)

1   *(The scene takes place in MIKE's car. Four young men,*
2   *MIKE, KENNY, CHUCK and PAUL, are parked, waiting for a*
3   *friend.)*
4   CHUCK: So, who's coming tonight?
5   MIKE: Everybody.
6   CHUCK: Everybody? What does that mean? Everybody?
7   KENNY: You invited everybody?
8   MIKE: I didn't invite anyone. Word gets around. People find
9   out when there's a party.
10   CHUCK: So you don't even know if anyone is coming.
11   KENNY: People are coming.
12   PAUL: How do you know if people are coming? I probably
13   chipped in for a ton of food that no one will be here to eat.
14   CHUCK: And this is a bad thing? Idiot.
15   PAUL: One of these days, Chuck, I'm going to really....
16   CHUCK: In your dreams, pussycat.
17   PAUL: Yeah...well...uh...
18   CHUCK: Don't tax yourself, OK, Paul? Move over, you're
19   crowding me.
20   PAUL: One of these days, I'm telling you....
21   CHUCK: What? What are you going to do?
22   PAUL: Just wait. One of these days...
23   CHUCK: You're amazing, you know that?
24   MIKE: Shut up and let's just get things ready. Paul, move over
25   so Chuck will quit whining.
26   KENNY: When did your parents leave?
27   MIKE: This morning.
28   KENNY: And they're gone till Monday? Awesome.
29   MIKE: And everybody will be here.
30   PAUL: Or nobody.
31   MIKE: Shut up, Paul.
32   PAUL: I mean it, one of these days....
33   CHUCK: You know, your grasp of the English language is
34   amazing. What's your native tongue?
35   KENNY: Leave him alone, Chuck.

1   MIKE: Kenny, you're spending the night, right?

2   KENNY: I thought I wouldn't be able to, but now I can.

3   MIKE: Good. Chuck, Paul, how about you two?

4   CHUCK: All over it.

5   PAUL: I thought we all were.

6   MIKE: Cool. Dammit, where is Doug? He said he'd meet us

7   here to help get stuff ready for tonight.

8   KENNY: I thought I saw him in Heidi's car.

9   MIKE: Heidi? No way.

10 KENNY: Yeah. They weren't talking though, or at least it

11   didn't look like they were talking. Heidi was driving

12   pretty fast. She's coming tonight, right?

13 CHUCK: That girl is crazy.

14 MIKE: Yeah, but she's funny.

15 PAUL: Hey, if Gina comes, she's mine tonight.

16 CHUCK: She's yours? What do you mean she's yours? Did you

17   tag her? Is she wearing one of those tracking devices?

18 PAUL: I told you last week, jerk, that if I had the chance to be

19   with Gina I was going to take it. Well, tonight is my chance.

20 KENNY: Have fun. I've been there and done that.

21 PAUL: Shut up! You have not.

22 KENNY: Heck, yeah, long time ago. Watch out, she's a lipper.

23 PAUL: Excuse me?

24 CHUCK: Lipper, huh?

25 MIKE: I hate that.

26 KENNY: You don't understand, it was like the whole night.

27 PAUL: What do you mean, "lipper"?

28 MIKE: When was this?

29 KENNY: I told you. Remember, after Tiffany's party? I told

30   you she lipped me...

31 PAUL: What's "lipped"? What's a "lipper"?

32 MIKE: Oh, yeah...

33 CHUCK: I couldn't figure out what was going on back there...

34 KENNY: Oh, yeah, that was in your car, huh? That was funny...

35 PAUL: Is anyone going to tell me about lipping?

1   KENNY: The girl takes your lip in her mouth and practically
2   swallows it.
3   PAUL: Your lip? Singular?
4   KENNY: Yeah. Bottom lip and *(Making a sucking, swallowing*
5   *sound) swwwiiippp.*
6   PAUL: That could be kind of exciting.
7   MIKE: Maybe the first ten minutes or so, but after awhile it
8   got old...
9   KENNY: I thought we'd have to be surgically removed from
10   one another. It was annoying. After about twenty
11   minutes, I finally told her I had to get going.
12   MIKE: She's a lousy kisser, too.
13   CHUCK: Oh, yeah! She tries way too hard.
14   PAUL: Wait a minute, you've all macked with her?
15   ALL THREE: *(A look of annoyed surprise, then)* Yeah.
16   PAUL: Then, dammit, she's mine tonight. I will be lipped
17   tonight! *(Pause)*
18   MIKE: You saw Doug?
19   KENNY: I told you I did.
20   MIKE: When?
21   KENNY: I don't know.
22   CHUCK: I'm getting hungry.
23   MIKE: Leave the food alone, Chuck.
24   CHUCK: What? I didn't say I wanted any.
25   PAUL: *(Mocking)* I'm getting hungry. *(Normal voice)* What was
26   that?
27   CHUCK: What? A man can't be hungry? It's a crime now to
28   express a bodily need? I made a simple statement and
29   you go off. You're really beginning to annoy me, you
30   know that, Paul?
31   PAUL: One of these days...
32   CHUCK: If you say that one more time, I swear to God I will...
33   PAUL: Oneofthesedays! Oneofthesedays! Oneofthesedays!
34   Oneofthesedays!
35   CHUCK: *(Going for him)* That's it! That's it!

1   **KENNY: Both of you knock it off. Idiots!** *(To MIKE)* **Why did we**
2   **bring them? I told you they'd act like fools.** *(Back to PAUL*
3   *and CHUCK)* **I'm not going to tell you again, knock this**
4   **crap off.**
5   **CHUCK:** *(Sarcastically)* **OK, Mommy.** *(After a silent moment to*
6   *PAUL, quietly)* **Loser.**
7   **PAUL:** *(Just as quietly)* **...One of these days...** *(They start to fight*
8   *again.)*
9   **MIKE: That's it, out of the car.**
10   **CHUCK: What?! What's wrong?**
11   **PAUL: C'mon, Mike, don't be a jerk.**
12   **MIKE: You two are the jerks. You're back there like kids.**
13   **CHUCK: I think you're missing the obvious here, Mike. We**
14   **are kids.**
15   **KENNY: Shut up, all of you. God!** *(They sit silently for a*
16   *moment.)* **Look, there's Rhonda. She's good to go from**
17   **the neck down, yeah?**
18   **MIKE: Oh, yeah. Put a bag over her head and I'd take any part**
19   **of that.**
20   **KENNY: I'd say so. Very definitely. Fine butt. I'm a butt man,**
21   **always have been.**
22   **PAUL: Really? I am attracted to eyes. I'm a sensitive kind of**
23   **guy, you know?**
24   **CHUCK: Are you? So, do you still hang out at the bottom of**
25   **Splash Mountain at Disneyland to see the girls in their**
26   **wet T-shirts, Paul?**
27   **PAUL: Ahhh, the good old days. But, no, I've moved beyond**
28   **that kind of infantile behavior.**
29   **CHUCK: Yeah? Still have your Disneyland year-round**
30   **passport?**
31   **PAUL: Don't need it. Women see that I am sensitive. They love**
32   **that kind of thing.**
33   **CHUCK: And in what parellel universe is this, my friend?**
34   **PAUL: Hey, I get my share of dates. I get around. Unlike some**
35   **of you losers, I just don't talk about the women I go**

1   out with.

2 CHUCK: Yeah. Sure. And if you had the amount of dates you'd

3   like us to believe you had, you'd be shouting it from the

4   rooftops.

5 PAUL: You don't know.

6 KENNY: He has a point, Paul. You haven't even macked with

7   Gina, and that is *ooolllddd* territory. Gina has a

8   nice butt.

9 CHUCK: You think?

10 MIKE: A-one butt. A fine butt. A classic, well-rounded, finely

11   sculpted butt. Yes, good buttage.

12 KENNY: I've got a nice butt.

13 MIKE: *(A slight and confused pause)* OK.

14 KENNY: No, I do. The way my leg curves in and leads perfectly

15   up to my butt. Pretty proud of that. I'm not being

16   conceited, just making a point. You're the one who

17   brought up butts.

18 MIKE: I was referring to Gina and Rhonda...

19 KENNY: I was just continuing on in the stream of the

20   conversation.

21 PAUL: You are one sick little puppy, Ken.

22 KENNY: OK, flat-butt.

23 PAUL: What?

24 KENNY: Your butt. It goes straight from your ankles to your

25   shoulders, no curves.

26 CHUCK: You've made a study of this? Have you looked at

27   my butt?

28 KENNY: I meant...What I'm saying is...Never mind, forget it.

29 MIKE: Paul, did you tell Jean about tonight?

30 PAUL: Uhhh...

31 CHUCK: Omigod, you did, didn't you? You are such an idiot...

32 PAUL: It wasn't my fault.

33 KENNY: *(Mocking)* It wasn't my fault. Then how did she find

34   out? Tell us, Paul, how did she find out?

35 PAUL: The same way everyone is finding out, they just do,

1   right, Mike?

2 MIKE: Don't bring me into this. That girl is crazy and I don't

3   want her at my house.

4 PAUL: So what was I supposed to say? "No, no party at Mike's.

5   Ignore all the cars in front of his house, you see no

6   people"? Come on, who knows what she would do to me

7   if I lied to her.

8 CHUCK: Is she the biggest bitch you have ever seen? The girl

9   is crazy. She scares me.

10 KENNY: Did you see her with Doug yesterday?

11 MIKE: She was with Doug?

12 KENNY: You don't even know! What is she, five one, five two at

13   the most? Doug, I swear to God, was shaking.

14 PAUL: What was she doing?

15 CHUCK: Making his life miserable, I hope. I can't stand that

16   guy.

17 KENNY: Are we going to sit here all day?

18 MIKE: I told you, Doug is meeting us here.

19 PAUL: Why are we waiting for him?

20 CHUCK: Is he the biggest moron in the world, or what?

21 MIKE: He's OK.

22 CHUCK: He's a jerk. I mean, I can be pretty vile, and if I'm

23   calling him a jerk, then he's really a jerk. He's a jerk.

24 PAUL: He used to beat me up regularly once a month in

25   elementary school.

26 KENNY: *(Laughing)* I remember that...Thursdays, wasn't it?

27 PAUL: I'm happy to know you have fond memories of that...

28 KENNY: Sorry...

29 CHUCK: You could set your clock by it.

30 MIKE: Why every Thursday once a month?

31 PAUL: Because, he'd beat me up on a Thursday, get

32   suspended, and have a three-day weekend. I was like his

33   holiday booking guide.

34 CHUCK: It got so that we'd all be waiting down by the

35   backstop on the lower baseball field every third

1   Thursday of the month.

2   KENNY: Why didn't you ever fight back?

3   PAUL: I did the first couple times, but then, after awhile I
4   realized that if I just let him beat me up, you know, just
5   stood there, he'd tire out and it would be over pretty
6   quick. Seemed like the logical thing to do.

7   CHUCK: Why'd he finally stop?

8   PAUL: You know, I don't know. After awhile he just did. Just
9   one day I showed up at the backstop and he wasn't there.
10   I actually waited for him. He never showed up.

11   CHUCK: It threw us all off schedule.

12   MIKE: You're a sensitive guy, Chuck, you know that, don't you?

13   KENNY: Well, I say we wait two more minutes then forget
14   him, we're outta here.

15   MIKE: Fine with me.

16   CHUCK: Sounds good.

17   PAUL: I'm used to waiting for Doug. I don't care either way.

18   KENNY: No wonder you're in therapy.

19   PAUL: Yeah, well. *(Silence ensues, broken only by the music*
20   *coming from the car stereo. Playing is a song all four of the*
21   *guys like and get into.)*

22   CHUCK: *(After the song)* OK, I say we leave.

23   MIKE: Fine with me. We'll catch him later.

24   KENNY: Hey, isn't that Gina over there?

25   CHUCK: I think it is. Hey, Gina, Paul wants to talk to you.

26   PAUL: *Shut up!* Drive, Mike, drive.

27   KENNY: Gina, Paul's in love with you.

28   PAUL: Omigod. Mike, I'm begging you, drive...

29   KENNY: Gina...

30   CHUCK: Gina... *(CHUCK and KENNY proceed to make obnoxious*
31   *slurping sounds, and MIKE begins to drive and PAUL drops*
32   *below eye level as we fade out.)*

33

34

35

The Last High School Party, Ever

(Scene for three women)

1	*(The scene takes place in the bathroom of MIKE's house the*
2	*night of his party. TIFFANY and LEAH enter for some*
3	*female bonding time with SUZANNE following shortly. The*
4	*voice outside the door should be that of a male.)*
5	**TIFFANY: Have you seen Jonathan tonight?**
6	**LEAH: Yes! What was that all about?**
7	**TIFFANY: I have no idea.**
8	**SUZANNE: What?**
9	**TIFFANY: He blew on me.**
10	**LEAH: Me, too. Right here on my face.**
11	**TIFFANY: Just on your face? He blew in my mouth.**
12	**SUZANNE: In your mouth?**
13	**TIFFANY: Yes. I could taste apple. Golden Delicious.**
14	**SUZANNE: You're lying.**
15	**TIFFANY: No, really. I think it was a Golden Delicious.**
16	**LEAH: He blowkissed me, too. It was the strangest thing. Do**
17	**you like my hair like this? I was thinking of cutting it.**
18	**TIFFANY: Cutting it? How short?**
19	**LEAH: Maybe to my shoulders. I don't know.**
20	**TIFFANY: How 'bout chin length?**
21	**SUZANNE: Jonathan is blowkissing? Where did he pick that up?**
22	**LEAH: I've heard of it, but no one has ever done it to me. Chin**
23	**length? Hmmm, that's kinda short.**
24	**TIFFANY: I feel violated. But somehow intrigued. I wouldn't**
25	**go any shorter than chin length.**
26	**SUZANNE: I'm going to find him.**
27	**LEAH: Why?**
28	**SUZANNE: I've never been blown on...I want to see what**
29	**it's like.**
30	**TIFFANY: Be warned, it's very weird.**
31	**SUZANNE: I'll be right back.** *(She exits.)*
32	**LEAH: Chin length? Maybe.**
33	**TIFFANY: At least get rid of the split ends.**
34	**LEAH: Yeah, I know. God, I love these parties.**
35	**TIFFANY: You do?**

1 LEAH: Yeah. They are so predictable, but there's still room for
2   the mystery of what will really happen.
3 TIFFANY: A predictable mystery?
4 LEAH: Oh, sure. Think about it. Some girl always gets in a
5   fight with her boyfriend and she takes off running down
6   the street and all of her friends have to chase after her
7   and calm her down, and his friends gather around him
8   and tell him that the girl is a bitch and then everyone gets
9   back together and makes stupid accusations at one
10   another and then different people pair up. Well, you
11   know...that's where the mystery is!
12 TIFFANY: Mystery. Great. The only thing that isn't a mystery
13   is that I will leave early.
14 LEAH: Why?
15 TIFFANY: I think I'm beyond this kind of party. I'm telling
16   you, the shallowness of some people is beginning to be a
17   bit much.
18 LEAH: Well, let's not talk about Suzanne while she's not in
19   the room. *(She examines her hair again.)* I do have split
20   ends, don't I? Darn, I cream rinse.
21 TIFFANY: I don't mean her. I mean all the rest of these people.
22 LEAH: Like who?
23 TIFFANY: Chuck, for instance.
24 LEAH: He's not so bad
25 TIFFANY: He's a jerk. So immature.
26 LEAH: Yeah, well...
27 A VOICE: Hey, there are other people who want to use this
28   bathroom.
29 LEAH: There are other bathrooms in the house. Find one.
30 A VOICE: They're all being used.
31 TIFFANY: Then go yell at them. We're busy in here.
32 A VOICE: I can't believe it!
33 LEAH: Whatever.
34 SUZANNE: *(Outside the door)* Excuse me, I'm going in there.
35 A VOICE: I was next.

1   SUZANNE: *(Still outside the door)* **Tough.** *(She enters.)* **Some**
2   **people!**
3   TIFFANY: **Did you find him?**
4   SUZANNE: **Yeah! He did it! I've been blowkissed. Right on the**
5   **lips. Tif, you're right, he does taste like apple. I'm looking**
6   **at the young man in a whole new light.**
7   TIFFANY: **You liked it?**
8   SUZANNE: **I like apple, OK?**
9   TIFFANY: **Uh-huh, I see.**
10   LEAH: **Well, I guess we know who Suzanne will be with this**
11   **evening.**
12   SUZANNE: **Could be.**
13   TIFFANY: **Not me. Leaving when the foolishness starts.**
14   LEAH: **Then you better plan on going soon, because you know**
15   **how these people act when there's a full moon.**
16   SUZANNE: **They act like idiots!**
17   TIFFANY: **There's got to be more to life than these stupid high**
18   **school parties.**
19   SUZANNE: **We just got here and you're already making**
20   **judgments? Lighten up. We only get a short while to go to**
21   **these silly parties. Let's enjoy it.**
22   TIFFANY: **It's been my experience that if you don't make**
23   **smart choices now, only dregs are left for you. I've had**
24   **dregs, I don't need it anymore. I've moved beyond dregs.**
25   **I deserve the cream of the crop.**
26   SUZANNE: **You *deserve* cream? How do you figure? You're**
27   **still a child.**
28   LEAH: **Hey, I've worked hard, I deserve the best of what life**
29   **has. And trust me, these parties are not what the best of**
30   **life has to offer.**
31   TIFFANY: **Oh, for heaven's sake, lighten up. It's just a party.**
32   LEAH: **It's the same old same old. You'll get together with**
33   **Kenny. And you are going for Mr. Golden Delicious.**
34   SUZANNE: **It's not set in stone.**
35   LEAH: **Girl, you have had your eye on him for weeks.**

1   TIFFANY: Totally.
2   SUZANNE: No! I have not. I certainly have not. No. OK, maybe
3   a little. But, good grief, he's so...I don't know...
4   LEAH: The man blowkisses! He's obviously picked up new
5   things from someone somewhere.
6   TIFFANY: Who knows what other treats he might have in
7   store for you?
8   LEAH: Oh, go on, give it a shot. And, of course, you will return
9   with the details.
10 SUZANNE: Of course.
11 LEAH: It will probably be the only excitement I get tonight.
12   Right now my biggest thrill is deciding the new length of
13   my hair. God, I am hating life.
14 TIFFANY: No, we'll fix you up with someone.
15 LEAH: Great, a P.K.
16 SUZANNE: Is Megan coming tonight?
17 LEAH: I don't know. She said that she was doing something
18   with Doug...
19 TIFFANY: I thought she hated Doug...
20 LEAH: Don't we all?
21 SUZANNE: Is he the biggest pig in the world or what?
22 A VOICE: I'm still waiting out here.
23 SUZANNE: Go away.
24 LEAH: Who is that, anyway?
25 SUZANNE: I care?
26 TIFFANY: We'll be out when we're done, OK!
27 A VOICE: Why are there three of you in there?
28 SUZANNE: Why do you think it's your business? Go away!
29 TIFFANY: Leah, listen, you can have Kenny if you want him.
30 LEAH: I can *have* him? Like your leftovers?
31 TIFFANY: You could do worse.
32 SUZANNE: She has.
33 LEAH: No, keep him. I can find someone on my own.
34 SUZANNE: Who?
35 LEAH: Please, I'm not so desperate that I will end up by

1   myself tonight. Maybe I'm just beyond it, you know?

2   There are plenty of guys out there, *if* I were interested.

3   TIFFANY: Yeah, like Chuck... *(She laughs derisively.)*

4   SUZANNE: Ohhh, let's talk about that...

5   LEAH: Let's not. I'm ready to go out to the party.

6   TIFFANY: Talk about what? *(SUZANNE smiles evilly.)*

7   LEAH: Shut up, Suzanne...

8   SUZANNE: Are you ashamed...

9   TIFFANY: What? Leah, you didn't?

10   SUZANNE: Not much she didn't...

11   LEAH: Is nothing sacred with you? Is there nothing I can tell

12   you in confidence that you won't run around telling

13   everyone?

14   TIFFANY: Leah, you went out with Chuck? With Chuck?

15   SUZANNE: Can you believe it?

16   LEAH: It was a weak moment. I was vulnerable.

17   A VOICE: Ladies!

18   ALL THREE: *Shut up!*

19   TIFFANY: Chuck! Omigod. How weak would I have to be to

20   mac with Chuck? I'd have to be close to death.

21   SUZANNE: You could be dead and that wouldn't stop Chuck

22   Thornton.

23   TIFFANY: Leah, what were you thinking? Were you mentally

24   disabled from studying for finals?

25   SUZANNE: She doesn't even have that for an excuse. Remem-

26   ber last Wednesday after we watched videos at Scott's?

27   TIFFANY: You got together with Chuck during the week?

28   Omigod.

29   LEAH: Suzanne, I can't believe you are telling her this...

30   SUZANNE: It gets better. Anyway, remember Chuck didn't

31   have a ride home, so he jumps in Leah's car?

32   TIFFANY: In your car? Omigod! I'd have the whole thing

33   disinfected immediately.

34   LEAH: I swear, Suzanne, you're dead...

35   SUZANNE: Somehow, it ends up that Chuck is the last one left

1   in the car to take home, so...

2   LEAH: Excuse me, but can I tell the story? I mean, if I am

3   going to be humiliated, at least let me do it in my own

4   way. Anyway, Chuck was in the car, and we were talking

5   and I pulled up to his house. You know, when he's by

6   himself, he's not so bad.

7   TIFFANY: Please...

8   LEAH: Can I finish, please? At any rate, we were talking and

9   he was so nice. And funny. And all of a sudden, he didn't

10   look so...

11   SUZANNE: Repulsive?

12   TIFFANY: Sickening?

13   SUZANNE: Nauseating?

14   TIFFANY: Hideous?

15   LEAH: He looked OK.

16   TIFFANY: Seeing him in the dark helped, too.

17   SUZANNE: Blindfolded would be better.

18   LEAH: I'm serious. He looked OK. Kinda cute in an offbeat not-

19   of-this-planet sort of way. It was so weird. I mean, here I

20   am, sitting with Chuck, of all people, and he's starting to

21   look good. And we're laughing and talking, and the time is

22   going by and I felt good about being there with him. Like

23   it was a side of him I've never seen. Then he said he had to

24   go in, and it just felt natural to hug him...

25   SUZANNE: Tiffany, look, my skin is starting to crawl.

26   LEAH: I'm serious.

27   TIFFANY: OK, a hug, but to go beyond that?

28   SUZANNE: I'm dizzy with disgust. Leah, tell her what you

29   told me.

30   LEAH: *(Mumbling)* Hmphs snoght abeed kyssr.

31   TIFFANY: What? What did she say?

32   SUZANNE: Leah, speak up. Tell her...

33   LEAH: *(Deep breath)* He's not a bad kisser, OK? He wasn't

34   awful. In fact, it was pretty good. Surprisingly good.

35   SUZANNE: Are you dying? I'm dying. And it wasn't just one

1   kiss, either, was it?

2   LEAH: OK. Shoot me.

3   SUZANNE: Or at least get her some antibiotics.

4   LEAH: In fact, I just might do it again tonight.

5   TIFFANY: God knows he'll be available.

6   LEAH: Listen, I don't want a relationship tonight. I just want

7   a nice, casual mac. And since I don't plan on ever

8   attending another high school party, Chuck is the perfect

9   choice. I'll just get him alone outside.

10 SUZANNE: Out of the sight of anyone who could hold it

11   against you...and your reputation...

12 TIFFANY: I am sitting here, stunned. I can't breathe. Look at

13   me, I'm hyperventilating.

14 LEAH: Yeah, well, don't knock it till you've tried it.

15 TIFFANY: I'll stick with Kenny. At least I know where he's been.

16 SUZANNE: I'm going for the blowkissing apple boy.

17 LEAH: Well, I feel like learning a lot more about Chuck. Find

18   your own rides home tonight, ladies. I'm taking Chuck

19   home...alone. Then I'm never going to another high

20   school party again.

21 TIFFANY: I will never be able to sit in that car again.

22 LEAH: And don't tell anyone! This is between us. *No one* must

23   ever find out that I am going with Chuck.

24 SUZANNE: Your secret is safe with me.

25 LEAH: It better be. *(Quick look in the mirror)* Chin length?

26   Yeah, maybe. Let's go.

27 A VOICE: *(As the door opens we see that it is CHUCK.)* Hey, I'm

28   not a bad kisser, huh?

29 LEAH: *(Slamming the door)* **OH, MY GOD!**

30

31

32

33

34

35

At the Party

(Scene for two men and two women)

1   *(RHONDA and GINA, KEVIN and COLE. The scene takes*
2   *place the night of MIKE's party in a living area.)*
3   **RHONDA: Well, another dull party. No unattached men left.**
4   **GINA: Did you see the way Tiffany zeroed in on Kenny? She**
5   **was like a swarm of locusts.**
6   **RHONDA: The girl is a plague.**
7   **GINA: So, do you want to hang around here alone without a**
8   **man worth spending time with or go to Cafe Coffee and**
9   **get some cappuccino?**
10   **RHONDA: I thought you said Kevin and Cole would be here.**
11   **GINA: That's what I heard.**
12   **RHONDA: Do you think they'd be interested in us?**
13   **GINA: Why not?**
14   **RHONDA: Hell, they probably already found someone to be**
15   **with tonight.**
16   **GINA: So, stay or go?**
17   **RHONDA: I don't know. It's awfully early to throw in the towel.**
18   **GINA: OK, we circle again, if we don't find anyone worth our**
19   **efforts, out we go.**
20   **RHONDA: Sounds good.** *(They exit.)*
21   **KEVIN: Cole, did you find anyone?**
22   **COLE: Nah. Even Leah is matched up.**
23   **KEVIN: No kidding! With who?**
24   **COLE:** *(A dramatic pause)* **Chuck.**
25   **KEVIN: Liar! God, are we a pair of losers or what? Even Chuck**
26   **has a partner. What do we have? Each other.**
27   **COLE: I don't know why we came to Mike's party. He's over by**
28   **the door acting like a cop. This is so boring. I thought you**
29   **said Gina and Rhonda would be here.**
30   **KEVIN: That's what I heard. Do you think they'd be interested**
31   **in us?**
32   **COLE: Why not. What's wrong with us?**
33   **KEVIN: Hell, they probably already found someone to be with**
34   **tonight.**
35   **COLE: The way our luck's been going, I don't doubt it.**

1   KEVIN: You wanna go?

2   COLE: Go where?

3   KEVIN: I don't know. The Cafe Coffee?

4   COLE: I hate coffee.

5   KEVIN: So do I, but there are usually some pretty hot girls there.

6   COLE: Nah.

7   KEVIN: Well, I guess we can just hang out here for a while.

8   COLE: Wouldn't you know, the one night my parents extend

9   my curfew and the only excitement I have is talking to

10   you about how we have nothing to do.

11   KEVIN: Tell me about it.

12   COLE: I say we circle the house, see if there is anyone who

13   isn't attached, try to find some small bit of fun or

14   excitement, and then get the hell out of here.

15   KEVIN: Right behind you. *(They exit.)*

16   GINA: Nothing.

17   RHONDA: No one.

18   GINA: I swear, you know you are a loser when even Chuck

19   starts to look good to you.

20   RHONDA: Did you see Jonathan and Brenna are together

21   again?

22   GINA: What's with that? I thought he was off to greener

23   pastures and new experiences?

24   RHONDA: Who knows with that boy?

25   GINA: Whatever. I say we're outahere.

26   RHONDA: I'm with you. Just let me get my jacket. *(She exits;*

27   *GINA stands aimlessly.)*

28   COLE: *(Entering)* OK, that's it. It's a sad day when Chuck

29   Thornton has someone and I stand alone.

30   KEVIN: Cole, there's Gina.

31   COLE: Where?

32   KEVIN: Over there.

33   COLE: Yes! I told you they'd be here.

34   KEVIN: Where's Rhonda? Gina and Rhonda are always

35   together.

1   COLE: Here she comes.

2   RHONDA: OK, I got my jacket. Let's make tracks.

3   GINA: Rhonda, there's Kevin and Cole. I told you they'd be here.

4   RHONDA: Where?

5   GINA: Over there, by the food.

6   COLE: Be cool. Don't act stupid. Are they looking at us?

7   KEVIN: They're looking in this direction. I can't tell if they

8   are looking *at* us, but they're looking.

9   COLE: So, what you are saying is we could be in their line of

10   vision.

11   KEVIN: Yeah.

12   COLE: Be cool. Don't look desperate.

13   KEVIN: Yeah, yeah. Don't look desperate. I'm cool. I'm very cool.

14   COLE: Me, too.

15   GINA: What is that on Cole's face?

16   RHONDA: I'm not wearing my glasses, I can't tell.

17   GINA: Why don't you wear the damn things?

18   RHONDA: At a party? Are you mad?

19   KEVIN: Wipe the dip off your chin.

20   COLE: Great! Did they see me with food on my face?

21   KEVIN: Probably not.

22   COLE: I'm cool.

23   GINA: Oh, it's gone now.

24   RHONDA: Are they looking at us?

25   GINA: I don't know. *(She waves.)*

26   COLE: Gina just waved.

27   KEVIN: But did she wave at us?

28   COLE: Who else would she be waving at?

29   KEVIN: It could be anyone.

30   GINA: I waved, but they didn't respond. *(She flicks her hair*

31   *with her waving hand.)*

32   RHONDA: Good cover. No reason to embarrass ourselves.

33   COLE: Should I wave back?

34   KEVIN: Is her hand still in the wave position?

35   COLE: Wait! She's messing with her hair.

1   KEVIN: Idiot! You thought a hair motion was a wave. Moron!
2   COLE: I could have sworn she waved.
3   GINA: That Cole is so cute, don't you think?
4   RHONDA: I don't know, I kinda think Kevin is adorable.
5   KEVIN: Do you really think Gina and Rhonda would give us
6   the time of day?
7   COLE: What's wrong with us?
8   GINA: I wish they'd come over here.
9   RHONDA: Me, too.
10 KEVIN: They are so far out of our league it isn't even funny.
11   Besides, I heard Paul was going to get together with Gina
12   tonight. And Mike has Rhonda picked out.
13 COLE: Mike and Paul? We don't stand a chance.
14 RHONDA: Why don't they come over here?
15 GINA: I don't know. Smile at them.
16 RHONDA: Me? Why should I smile at them when they are so
17   obviously not interested?
18 GINA: Just do it.
19 RHONDA: Oh, God. *(She smiles in the boys' direction.)*
20 COLE: Omigod, Rhonda smiled at us!
21 KEVIN: The hell you say!
22 COLE: I swear on our friendship, Rhonda smiled at us. *(He*
23   *smiles back.)*
24 KEVIN: What are you doing?
25 COLE: Smiling back, what do you think?
26 RHONDA: So, did they smile back?
27 GINA: Cole looks like he's smiling.
28 KEVIN: Wait a minute. Rhonda's not wearing her glasses
29   tonight.
30 COLE: *(Immediately stops smiling.)* She's not? *(He quickly*
31   *looks in her direction.)* Oh, great!
32 GINA: Wait, he stopped smiling.
33 KEVIN: She was probably just giving the party smile to the
34   general population.
35 RHONDA: He stopped?

1 COLE: *(He covers his mouth.)* **Give me a toothpick.**
2 KEVIN: **Why?**
3 COLE: **So I can pretend my smile was a mouth maneuver to**
4   **get something out of my teeth.**
5 KEVIN: **Good idea, good idea.**
6 GINA: **Oh, he wasn't smiling. He's using a toothpick. He must**
7   **have had food in his teeth or something.**
8 RHONDA: **Damn.**
9 COLE: **Damn.** *(He and KEVIN stand picking their teeth for a*
10   *moment.)*
11 GINA: **Look at them with the toothpicks. They look so cool.**
12   **There is something so masculine about a man with a**
13   **toothpick.**
14 RHONDA: **Yeah, I know.**
15 KEVIN: **Ow!**
16 COLE: **What's wrong?**
17 KEVIN: **Splinter.** *(Wincing in pain)*
18 COLE: **Ooooh, that hurts.** *(Winces in sympathetic pain.)*
19 GINA: **I love the way their mouths scrunch up like that. So**
20   **kissable.**
21 RHONDA: **So sexy.**
22 KEVIN: **Great, I've probably started some sort of mouth**
23   **infection. Am I bleeding?**
24 COLE: **I don't know! What, do you want me to check?**
25 RHONDA: **So, what are we going to do, stand here all night?**
26 GINA: **I don't know. I'm getting tired.** *(She stretches.)*
27 COLE: **Be still my heart. Look at Gina, look at her.**
28 RHONDA: *(Stretching as well)* **Me, too.**
29 KEVIN: **Oh, help me, Rhonda, help, help me, Rhonda.**
30 GINA: **Well, it's pretty clear that Kevin and Cole just aren't**
31   **interested in us. Maybe we should go.**
32 RHONDA: **Probably. Everyone is going to be paired up pretty**
33   **soon and here we'll be, standing.**
34 KEVIN: **It will never happen. It's clear they're just not**
35   **interested.**

1   GINA: Well, at least one good thing came out of this night.
2   RHONDA: What?
3   GINA: I tried Jonathan's new kissing technique.
4   RHONDA: His blowkissing? Yeah, Suzanne told me.
5   GINA: Apparently he's giving visual aid demonstrations on
6   his new style. I tried it. You should.
7   KEVIN: You know Jonathan, he'd kiss a toad if you put it in
8   a dress.
9   COLE: I heard that Gina is a lipper.
10 KEVIN: That's what Kenny said.
11 GINA: I like the way I kiss. I love men with full lips. And look
12   at Cole's lips. Yum.
13 COLE: I wonder what that would be like?
14 GINA: I'll never get to try kissing him, though. He is just not
15   interested.
16 COLE: Well, I guess I'll never know. She's just not interested.
17 RHONDA: Kevin is the one I'm interested in.
18 KEVIN: Look at Rhonda. She's gorgeous. Head to toe gorgeous.
19 COLE: Look at them, standing there. They must be waiting
20   for someone.
21 KEVIN: Who?
22 COLE: One thing is sure, it ain't us.
23 GINA: Why don't they come over here?
24 RHONDA: I may as well resign myself to a life alone.
25 KEVIN: I bet she's a great kisser.
26 RHONDA: We should just go over there.
27 COLE: Why are we standing here? Are we men or are we
28   mice? (*He starts to cross and then immediately stops,*
29   *bending down like he dropped something.*)
30 GINA: Here comes Cole! Oh, no, he just dropped something
31   and picked it up.
32 KEVIN: Have some cheese, Ratboy.
33 RHONDA: Why don't we go over there?
34 GINA: Because it would be forward. It wouldn't look right. It
35   would be cheap.

1 RHONDA: So instead we spend yet another evening without a
2   man.
3 COLE: I was going, but I dropped this, uh, this...um...
4 KEVIN: Piece of lint?
5 COLE: I thought it was...never mind. I don't see you making
6   any moves.
7 KEVIN: I still have some pride.
8 RHONDA: Why don't we go over? Come on.
9 GINA: You think?
10 COLE: Yeah, pride can keep you real warm on a cold winter
11   night.
12 RHONDA: I'm going over there.
13 GINA: Yeah, do it.
14 RHONDA: Come on.
15 GINA: Me? No way. I don't need that kind of humiliation.
16 RHONDA: What's the worst that could happen?
17 GINA: They could be completely rude, walk away, sneer at us.
18 KEVIN: If they were interested in us, they would have come
19   over here. If we go over there and corner them, it would
20   be like sexual harassment or something.
21 COLE: I can see how it would be irritating to them, especially
22   if they are waiting for some other guys.
23 RHONDA: Let's give it a chance.
24 GINA: Look, Rhonda, they are probably waiting for some
25   other girls. You honestly think guys like Kevin and Cole
26   would be unattached this long? Think it through.
27 RHONDA: Good point.
28 COLE: Forget it. Let's circle one more time and then we're
29   outta here.
30 KEVIN: OK, but if we come back and they are still standing
31   there, let's go for it.
32 COLE: Only if they are still standing there and it's just the two
33   of them. Even if it's just another girl with them, I say
34   forget it.
35 GINA: If you're going to go over there, I guess I'll go with you.

1   KEVIN: OK. If Rhonda and Gina are still standing there, we
2   go over.
3   COLE: OK. Let's circle. *(They exit.)*
4   RHONDA: Where are they going?
5   GINA: I knew it. I *knew* it. They're with someone.
6   RHONDA: Well, that was close. I can just see us. "Hi, guys,
7   whatcha doin'?" "Oh, we've got some truly beautiful
8   women meeting us by the cheese dip and you're blocking
9   our view."
10 GINA: Thank God we didn't go over there earlier.
11 RHONDA: Well, another wasted Saturday night.
12 GINA: I'm so glad we came to this party. I know I needed this
13   shot of embarrassment before the evening was out.
14 RHONDA: Let's go. Maybe we'll meet someone at Cafe Coffee.
15 GINA: I hate coffee.
16 RHONDA: We're not going for the coffee. We're going for the
17   company.
18 GINA: Great, you and a cup of bitter hot liquid. Terrific.
19 RHONDA: Well, thank you so much.
20 GINA: Never mind, I take that back. You're the only free
21   human being left on this night. I don't want to mess that
22   up. My car or yours?
23 RHONDA: Yours. Hey, maybe there'll be a couple of cute
24   guys there.
25 GINA: Yeah! And maybe I'll grow wings and fly to Jupiter. God,
26   what a crummy night. *(They exit.)*
27 COLE: *(Entering)* I told you they'd be gone.
28 KEVIN: Great. I knew we should have gone over there when
29   we had the chance.
30 COLE: So, what now?
31 KEVIN: Cafe coffee?
32 COLE: I hate coffee.
33 KEVIN: Then just sit there and drink it and we'll talk about
34   what a pair of losers we are.
35 COLE: Another fun Saturday night.

1   KEVIN: Maybe we'll find some cute girls there.
2   COLE: You know, you really have to stop living in this fantasy
3   life.
4   KEVIN: My car or yours?
5   COLE: Mine. God, what a crummy night. *(They exit.)*
6
7
8
9
10
11
12
13
14
15
16
17
18
19
20
21
22
23
24
25
26
27
28
29
30
31
32
33
34
35

Weapons

(Monolog for one woman)

1 (*SHERYL is getting ready for MIKE's party and during her*
2 *conversation does her hair and makeup.*)
3 SHERYL: I call these my weapons. This blush is one of those
4 kinds that has two tones of peachy rose for accenting the
5 cheekbones. I've got the kind of coloring that if I go with
6 peachy I look jaundiced, and if I go with rose I look like
7 some kind of cheap tart, so if I mix the two I get just the
8 right amount of fresh and natural non-make-uppy look.
9 Natural fiber blush brush, too. No polyester here! Eye
10 liner in two shades, brown and dark brown. You don't
11 want black because it's way too harsh. But if you go with
12 light brown you might as well not wear any at all, so
13 what's the point? And you have to use the pencil because
14 the liquid stuff smears and wiggles. But don't put it on
15 too thick, because if you do it defeats the purpose of
16 enlarging the eye. Start at the middle of the eye and go
17 outward. It's a matter of practice, that's all. And don't
18 forget about mascara, thick lash, of course. But you have
19 to be careful with the mascara because if you get the
20 cheap stuff it gets all clumpy and makes you look like
21 Tammy Faye, may God forbid. I spend a lot of money on
22 mascara because my eyes are my best feature and you
23 can't cheat on the lashes. The rest of this stuff I get at the
24 dollar counter at the Pic and Save. To be honest, it's all
25 pretty much the same. Except the mascara. It's
26 important to remember the difference. I get mine at
27 Nordstrom's. I know it's extravagant, but think about it.
28 So I spend an extra two or three dollars and I have the
29 satisfaction of knowing that my eyes will look great. It's
30 sort of like a little insurance policy. I hope you're paying
31 attention. The lips are important, too. Very important,
32 especially on a night like tonight. You want to have color,
33 but you don't want it to make a mess if you get together
34 with someone. I usually go with a strawberry gloss. You
35 don't want to get the kind in a pot that you put on with

1 your fingers because then you get all icky and where do
2 you wipe your hands and it's always a mess. Nope. You get
3 this stuff at the Pic and Save, right at the counter, and
4 you can't go wrong. It comes in this handy little tube that
5 fits perfectly in your pocket. Not only that, it's soft and
6 flexible, so if you are wearing something that doesn't
7 have pockets, you can stick it in your bra, which is an
8 asset, because then it stays warm and goes on easier. And
9 always wear a bra. Trust me, you'll regret it later if you
10 don't. Look at all those women from the sixties and
11 seventies who didn't. Sag city. Pitiful.

12 Mike's party tonight is supposed to be a very big deal,
13 so I want to look good. Everyone will be there. We've all
14 been waiting a long time for a party like this, our last
15 party before we all graduate. His parents are gone, but it
16 won't be rowdy because we're not the kind of kids to be
17 stupid. We have respect for Mike's home and his parents'
18 faith in him. So, it won't be like Chuck's party was where
19 the whole football team came and drank and proceeded
20 to act like fools and tear up the house. That was awful,
21 really awful. Of course, look at Chuck. He's like a walking
22 advertisement for teenage evil. He was right in the
23 middle of all that, encouraging it. And when his parents
24 got home and saw that disaster, they didn't do anything
25 about it. Just called in some professional house cleaners,
26 had the carpets replaced and repaired the guest toilet in
27 the downstairs bathroom. I don't know what happens to
28 teenage guys when they get too much beer in them. It
29 must be some sort of testosterone thing that I just don't
30 understand. But at Mike's it will be a lot better. Yeah,
31 everyone is invited. Well, I mean, everyone knows about
32 this party, but that doesn't mean it will be some big
33 blowout. Just a lot of nice people mingling and stuff.
34 There will be a few people there that I really want to see,
35 and some that I really want to see me. That's why I need

43

1 my weapons. And that's why I'm taking my time putting
2 this stuff on. I want to look beautiful, but not made up,
3 see? Which reminds me, never ever wear face makeup,
4 like powder or pancake or any of that. You only wear face
5 makeup when you are on stage or you're old and have a
6 lot of wrinkles to hide, like when you're thirty. You want
7 to look natural, kissable. The last thing a guy wants to see
8 is your face melting off onto his shirt. A real turn off,
9 trust me.

10 Anyway, I figure this is going to be about the last high
11 school party I go to. I've been going to high school parties
12 since I was in junior high. That's five years of high school
13 parties. (It's kind of weird to think that some of the guys
14 I got together with when I was a freshman are now
15 graduating from college. Hmmm.) Anyway, I want to look
16 really good for this last party. So I hope you don't mind if
17 I finish getting ready while I talk. I have all this worked
18 out to a science. See, if I just follow a simple plan of
19 attack I can be fully made up and looking pretty damn
20 good in just about eleven minutes. Not bad! I know some
21 girls take all day to get ready. Pathetic. There's so much
22 more to do in life than primp, you know? But some
23 people, I guess, just find it necessary to spend all day in
24 front of a mirror doing something that shouldn't take
25 more than a couple minutes.

26 Do you like this outfit? I do, even though it's jeans. I
27 know some girls don't like to wear jeans. Heather won't
28 even wear pants. "Girls wear dresses, boys wear pants,"
29 that's what she always says. But I'm perfectly
30 comfortable in a good pair of nice-fitting jeans. And jeans
31 are a good thing to wear, a good basic. You can look like a
32 slob in jeans, but take those very same jeans, put on a
33 nice button-down shirt and a blazer, and if you're feeling
34 really funky, a thin tie and tuck those jeans into some
35 black boots and you look very good. Want to look classy?

1 Same outfit, add a pair of earrings and put your hair up
2 and, voila', you are right off the cover of **YM** magazine.
3 Never, though, wear heels with jeans. Hello, tramp! if you
4 do. Trust me on this one.

5 A lot of people are going to be at this party tonight. It
6 should be pretty fun. But since this is my last appearance
7 at a high school party, I want to make an impression that
8 will last. God, I hate to think I'd turn into one of those
9 losers that keep going to high school parties after they
10 graduate. I'm counting on the fact that Nick Carloti will
11 be there. In fact, I bet you solid money that Nick will be
12 there. He graduated, what, four years ago? I remember,
13 and God this is embarrassing to admit, but I remember
14 being so impressed with myself for macking with him
15 when he was a senior and I was a freshman. I thought he
16 was the beginning and end of the world. Now, it's just
17 humiliating to think about it. I mean, look at him. He's
18 been out of school for four years and he's doing exactly
19 the same thing he did when he was in high school. A lot
20 of talk about all the things he's going to do, but never any
21 action to get him there. It's sad, really.

22 Nick, however, is one of the reasons I want to look
23 especially good tonight. Boy, did he use me four years
24 ago. Took advantage of my innocent nature. I'm not
25 saying we did anything more than mac, because we
26 didn't. I was young and stupid, but not a fool. What he
27 did was play with my feelings, lead me into thinking that
28 there was going to be a real relationship there. God, I was
29 dumb. I mean, really, what would a popular senior like
30 Nick see in a little freshman like me? Oh, he'd tell me
31 how he loved me and there was no one else. And, yeah, I
32 knew in my brain he was lying, but in my heart I wanted
33 to believe it. First love, you know? Even some of the
34 senior girls took me aside and told me what a cheating
35 worm he was and what he was doing. But would I listen?

45

1 No siree, not me. I told them that that's how he used to
2 be, but I would change him. Dumb, huh? But I learned a
3 really good lesson, you know. I learned that people are
4 who they are and they are not going to change. You either
5 love someone for who they are or move on. I can thank
6 Nick for that. He was a good learning experience. He was
7 fun, but he was a jerk and didn't really care about anyone
8 but himself. I learned that that's not the kind of person I
9 want in my life. A good lesson to learn early, rather than
10 waiting until you're in your twenties and marrying an
11 idiot hoping he'll turn into a decent person. 'Cause they
12 won't. But the nasty little vindictive side of me wants
13 Nick to see that the little girl whose mind he messed with
14 is now a grown woman.

15 Here's my plan. I am going to walk into that party
16 looking so fine that all heads will turn. See, this is the
17 perfect outfit to wear, too. Casual enough to look like I
18 just threw something together, but smart enough to look
19 stylish and stunning. And I'll tell you, jogging five miles
20 every day does wonders for the fit of your jeans! So, I will
21 sashay right up to Nick, give him a big hug and ask how
22 he's doing. He, of course, will tell me about how things
23 are just about coming together for him. How he's going to
24 start going on auditions for agents or he's thinking about
25 getting back into singing. You know, the same old same
26 old he's always talking about. Of course, he won't ask me
27 about what I'm doing, but I'll work the conversation
28 around to me eventually. OK, look at me. Hair, makeup,
29 outfit. I look great, right? My weapons are all in place. I'm
30 looking pretty devastating if I do say so myself. But!
31 Here's the atomic bomb that I am going to drop on him.
32 You ready?! I just found out today that I got accepted to
33 Yale! Ha! Yale! And I got a couple of scholarships that will
34 cover most of the costs. And I did it all with my own
35 talents, determination and brains. I'm going to *Yale!*

1　　　　My point here is this: Nick and I had the same four
2　　years. What has he done? Not much. Stagnated, works as
3　　a waiter in the same place he did four years ago. Talked a
4　　good game, but never got off the bench to play it. But in
5　　those same four years I worked hard and it paid off. It
6　　paid off big. That's the main weapon I have. Me! So, yeah,
7　　I do the makeup, hair and clothes thing. But I have a
8　　future that includes more than just looking good.
9　　Everything I do is up to me. And that, my young friend, is
10　　the best weapon of all.
11
12
13
14
15
16
17
18
19
20
21
22
23
24
25
26
27
28
29
30
31
32
33
34
35

Perspectives on PREGNANCY

Catching Up

(Scene for two women)

1   *(ANGIE visits her friend JUDY and her newborn baby.)*

2   ANGIE: He's just so cute.

3   JUDY: Yeah, he is, isn't he?

4   ANGIE: His eyes are so blue. He's got my favorite
5   combination, dark hair, blue eyes. He's going to be a little
6   heartbreaker, you just watch.

7   JUDY: Well, he's already gotten a strong hold on my heart.
8   From the minute I first saw him, I fell forever in love.

9   ANGIE: I don't blame you. He's adorable.

10   JUDY: Yeah, he is. But I'm prejudiced, I'm his mommy.

11   ANGIE: I know. Look at you! You are handling this so well. I
12   always knew you would.

13   JUDY: Thanks. It's been hard, but worth it.

14   ANGIE: And I can't believe how great you look.

15   JUDY: Not bad, huh? My waistline just snapped right back
16   into place.

17   ANGIE: It really did.

18   JUDY: I swear, I had so many people telling me how hard it
19   would be to get my figure back after the baby, but it
20   wasn't that hard.

21   ANGIE: Hey, that Abflex and the gym are terrific things, huh?

22   JUDY: Just plain old sit-ups.

23   ANGIE: Just sit-ups? You didn't use any of the machines at
24   the gym?

25   JUDY: No gym, either. Can't afford it.

26   ANGIE: Why?

27   JUDY: Other things take priority now, you know? Baby food,
28   diapers, formula, rent, utilities. All that stuff.

29   ANGIE: Whoa. I thought your parents were going to help you
30   and Tony out with things.

31   JUDY: They are a little bit. But, face it, they weren't that
32   thrilled to have their seventeen-year-old daughter "with
33   child." Their attitude seems to be that if I am going to
34   do adult things then I should take responsibility for
35   those actions.

1 ANGIE: That's a little harsh. They won't at least pay for the
2   membership at the gym?
3 JUDY: Hey, I'm happy when they throw in for some Pampers.
4   Those things are a fortune. I can't expect them to pay for
5   luxuries.
6 ANGIE: I hardly consider my membership at Fitness Center a
7   luxury.
8 JUDY: Well, for you it's not. For me, Tony, and now Brian,
9   something like that falls into the category of unnecessary.
10   Necessaries include toilet paper and Cheerios.
11 ANGIE: I don't know how you do it. You are so brave.
12 JUDY: It's not a matter of brave. You do what you have to do.
13 ANGIE: But you didn't have to do this.
14 JUDY: I know. And trust me, it hasn't been easy, Angie. But I
15   think that in the long run, I made the right choice. For me.
16 ANGIE: I guess. Well... *(There is an uncomfortable pause.)* Oh, I
17   know what I wanted to tell you. You will die! Casey
18   Powers asked Dana Porter out!
19 JUDY: No! You will shut up right now! He didn't!
20 ANGIE: Oh, but he did.
21 JUDY: Shut up! He has no business going out with that child.
22   What is she, fourteen?
23 ANGIE: Barely. Imagine, a freshman girl dating a senior guy.
24   A graduated senior guy.
25 JUDY: Has he lost his mind? And her. Do her parents know?
26 ANGIE: They are encouraging it!
27 JUDY: Well, what do you expect? His family has money and
28   social position and hers has nothing.
29 ANGIE: Obviously no pride, either
30 JUDY: This will lead to nothing good, trust me.
31 ANGIE: I bet she ends up in trouble, her kind always do... *(She*
32   *sees JUDY's stricken look.)* Oh, Judy, I didn't mean...God,
33   I've got a big mouth.
34 JUDY: Don't worry about it. Really. I know you didn't mean
35   anything.

1   ANGIE: I didn't. Sometimes my mouth is miles ahead of my
2   brain.
3   JUDY: *(A beat)* So what else is going on with everyone.
4   ANGIE: Well...ummm. Oh, I know! Guess who Brandy is going
5   out with!
6   JUDY: Brandy is going out with Robert.
7   ANGIE: Old news! She left Robert three months ago. She's
8   now going out with David!
9   JUDY: David who?
10   ANGIE: David! David, the new guy who came to school this
11   year. You know. Blond hair, cheekbones to spare and
12   shoulders enough for two men. The surfer.
13   JUDY: When did he come to school?
14   ANGIE: In October. Don't you remember? We were in line at
15   lunch and he came in with Josh that day before progress
16   reports came out and I was freaking because I was
17   getting a D in Spanish and then I saw him, and all
18   thoughts of Spanish disappeared and were replaced by
19   thoughts of David. You were there. Remember?
20   JUDY: No. Of course, that was right around when I thought I
21   was pregnant, so I guess I had other things going on in
22   my mind.
23   ANGIE: Still, I don't see how you could forget him.
24   JUDY: Well, I left school around then. I was getting sick all the
25   time.
26   ANGIE: Oh, yeah.
27   JUDY: Plus I had to take care of a lot of things. Doctors and
28   getting married and finding us a place to live that was
29   cheap enough so that Tony could still go to college and
30   just work part-time. Speaking of which, I need to get
31   ready pretty soon. I have to go to work.
32   ANGIE: You still cleaning houses?
33   JUDY: Yeah. The perfect job. I can set my own hours and take
34   little Brian with me. The pay isn't bad either. It's enough
35   where Tony can still do what he needs to do and the bills

1   pretty much get paid.
2 ANGIE: That's good. Really, it is. *(Another uncomfortable*
3   *silence)* So, what's new with you?
4 JUDY: Not a lot. Wait, finish telling me about Brandy and this
5   new guy. I never get to hear any of the good gossip. I don't
6   really get to see anyone much anymore.
7 ANGIE: Oh! Yeah, OK. Well, anyway, Brandy was at Mark's
8   going-away party...
9 JUDY: Going away? Where's he going?
10 ANGIE: I told you, he got accepted into Northwestern.
11 JUDY: Oh, that's right. That's where I had planned on going...
12 ANGIE: Yeah, I know.
13 JUDY: Yeah...so, anyway, Mark had his party.
14 ANGIE: Didn't you know about Mark's party?
15 JUDY: I don't hear much about parties. No one seems to
16   invite me.
17 ANGIE: You could have come.
18 JUDY: And brought Brian?
19 ANGIE: You could leave him with a sitter.
20 JUDY: Everyone who babysits are people my own age, and
21   they were probably all at Mark's party anyway.
22 ANGIE: I'm sure there's someone.
23 JUDY: It's a little hard getting a sitter, OK?
24 ANGIE: Oh. Yeah, I guess it would be.
25 JUDY: OK, Mark, party, Brandy, Northwestern, what else?
26 ANGIE: Well, Brandy walked in with David...
27 JUDY: The surfer...
28 ANGIE: The surfer, and who should also walk in but René!
29 JUDY: You lie!
30 ANGIE: I don't!
31 JUDY: Oh my God! René! Even I remember the fight they got
32   into last summer over Robert.
33 ANGIE: Well, they both must have remembered it, too,
34   because they re-enacted it right there in the middle of
35   Mark's mother's designer living room.

1   JUDY: You are not serious.

2   ANGIE: But yes! Hair flying, nails scratching, clothes tearing.

3   It was amazing.

4   JUDY: Remember last summer when they had that fight?

5   Brandy just reached right into René's car window and

6   punched her in the face.

7   ANGIE: Well, I could kind of understand that because René was

8   just stupid. I'm sorry, but you don't call someone a bitch

9   from your car when you are stuck in parking lot traffic.

10   JUDY: I will never forget that. René shows up that night at her

11   graduation with a big old black eye.

12   ANGIE: Well, she's got a matching one now! *(They laugh at the*

13   *memory.)*

14   JUDY: *(A beat)* Last summer seems so long ago.

15   ANGIE: You think? Seems like yesterday to me. But now here

16   we all are, ready to go off our own separate ways. Mark to

17   Northwestern, me to Boston, Derek to Wheaton, even

18   Brandy is going away to college.

19   JUDY: No way!

20   ANGIE: Yes! She's going to San Diego.

21   JUDY: State or University?

22   ANGIE: Hello! What do you think?

23   JUDY: Party school...State.

24   ANGIE: Right!

25   JUDY: I was going to go to Northwestern.

26   ANGIE: I know.

27   JUDY: Imagine, me and Mark together...

28   ANGIE: You guys were really good in the musical last year.

29   JUDY: Yeah, we were. God, all those seniors were so jealous of

30   the two juniors who got the leads in *West Side Story*. Is

31   Mark still going to major in theatre?

32   ANGIE: Oh, yeah. That's what he wants to do with his life.

33   JUDY: They've got a really good theatre program there, you

34   know.

35   ANGIE: Yeah.

1   JUDY: Theatre major. Seems like a stupid idea now.
2   ANGIE: It's not. You were good, Jud, really good. What other
3   high school junior was selected to represent State at the
4   Shakespeare Conference? And won it?
5   JUDY: I still have that trophy around here somewhere. My
6   mom packed it for me, but I haven't had time to look for it.
7   ANGIE: You should put it up where you can see it. To remind
8   you how good you were.
9   JUDY: Yeah, I was, huh? But that was then. I haven't acted
10   since my junior year. Now here I am with a baby. A trophy
11   for acting, a 1250 on my SAT score, a folder of letters of
12   recommendation for colleges, an overall 3.8 GPA and a
13   baby. Somewhere along the way, things got a little
14   messed up.
15 ANGIE: Yeah.
16 JUDY: I'm never going to college. I'm never going to be an
17   actress. I'm stuck.
18 ANGIE: I thought you were OK with all this. I thought you
19   were happy.
20 JUDY: Happy is a relative term. I'm as happy as I can be with
21   a really crummy situation that I never asked for.
22 ANGIE: Come on, it's not so bad.
23 JUDY: No? You know the last time I went out? The last time I
24   saw anybody from school? At my baby shower.
25 ANGIE: You've seen your friends. They've come over.
26 JUDY: Yeah, like you have. To see the baby and then to leave.
27 ANGIE: I'm not leaving.
28 JUDY: But you will pretty soon. You'll be leaving for Boston,
29   everyone will be leaving for college, Mark is going to *my*
30   college! And even Brandy of all people is going to college.
31   And I'll be stuck in this crummy little town with a baby
32   and a husband and no future.
33 ANGIE: But you love your baby. And Tony.
34 JUDY: Of course I love them. But that doesn't change how
35   I feel.

1   ANGIE: Do you wish you would have had the abortion?

2   JUDY: I wish I hadn't gotten myself into a situation that made

3   me make that decision. I wouldn't trade my baby for

4   anything, except maybe for some time.

5   ANGIE: What do you mean?

6   JUDY: Time to grow up, to go to college, to be an actress or a

7   teacher or something. But my choices are all gone now.

8   Oh, Tony can still do things. God knows he hasn't given

9   up a helluva lot. Why should he? He goes to college, he

10   works, but he comes and goes as he pleases. And I'm

11   stuck here with a baby and no future.

12   ANGIE: I didn't realize things were so bad. You seemed so

13   happy when I first got here.

14   JUDY: Of course I seemed happy. I'm happy for everyone's

15   benefit. The only person I cry in front of is little Brian. I

16   just hold him and cry. Someday when he's with what is

17   sure to be one in a long line of therapists, he will have

18   that repressed memory surface of his mother crying.

19   ANGIE: I'm so sorry.

20   JUDY: Don't be. It was my choice. I swear, though, I never

21   thought past the baby shower. It was all going to be so

22   much fun. Once I got over the initial shock of being

23   pregnant, it seemed so right. Everyone was so nice to me,

24   gifts for the baby, making a home for me and Tony. But

25   you know, I never thought past that baby shower. It was

26   like it was just another party with my friends. Then

27   Brian came and all of a sudden I found myself standing

28   all alone in the bathroom wiping baby spit off my

29   shoulder, smelling like diaper rash medicine, the baby

30   screaming in the next room and I looked in the mirror

31   and saw tears coming down my face. I never bargained

32   for this, that's for sure.

33   ANGIE: I don't know what to say.

34   JUDY: You can't say anything.

35   ANGIE: Well, look on the bright side. By the time Brian

1 graduates from high school and moves out, you'll only be
2 thirty-five. That's really young.
3 JUDY: Young? Compared to what?
4 ANGIE: In comparison to people that have kids at twenty-
5 seven. I mean, think about it. I probably won't get
6 married and have kids till I'm established in a career, so
7 figure about thirty. By the time my kids are grown and
8 gone, I'll be at least fifty. That's really old. I mean, you'll
9 have years in front of you to do all kinds of stuff. Think
10 of all that free time you'll have.
11 JUDY: So what you're saying is that I start on my life and
12 career when I'm thirty-seven. Which means being an
13 actress is out because actresses in their thirties are
14 considered old and used up...and I won't even have been
15 used at all.
16 ANGIE: You can go to college, you know.
17 JUDY: When?
18 ANGIE: When Brian starts school. You'll only be a few years
19 older than the other kids.
20 JUDY: You just don't understand. I've got enough to do here
21 taking care of the baby, cleaning houses to pay for Tony's
22 tuition, trying to study for my General Ed degree since I
23 had to drop out of high school.
24 ANGIE: I don't know what to tell you.
25 JUDY: You can't tell me anything. This is my life and I'm stuck
26 with it. I made choices that got me into this position and
27 now I have to live with them.
28 ANGIE: Judy, come to my house tonight.
29 JUDY: What for?
30 ANGIE: I'm having a little party. That's why I came over here
31 today. I wanted to invite you. I leave for Boston next
32 week, and I'd really like you to come tonight. Not a lot of
33 people, just close friends.
34 JUDY: You still think of me as a close friend?
35 ANGIE: I always will. Just because we don't hang out like we

1   used to doesn't mean I don't love you.

2   JUDY: What about Brian?

3   ANGIE: Can't Tony watch him?

4   JUDY: He's got a class tonight.

5   ANGIE: What about your parents?

6   JUDY: Oh, no. They made it really clear that they were not

7   going to be built-in babysitters. They want a week's

8   notice or they automatically say no.

9   ANGIE: Then bring him.

10   JUDY: Bring the baby?

11   ANGIE: Yeah. Why not? It's just a little party, no big deal.

12   Everyone would love to see you and the baby.

13   JUDY: Great, now I'm a side show attraction.

14   ANGIE: Don't be silly. Your friends want to see you. And Brian

15   is a part of you that isn't going away.

16   JUDY: I just wish he'd come about ten years later.

17   ANGIE: "And if wishes were horses…"

18   JUDY: "All men would ride." I know, I know.

19   ANGIE: Say you'll come.

20   JUDY: What time?

21   ANGIE: Dinner at six and then till whenever.

22   JUDY: And I can bring Brian?

23   ANGIE: I'd be mad if you didn't. And if he gets sleepy, we can

24   rig something up so he can nap.

25   JUDY: OK, I'll try.

26   ANGIE: Don't try. Do it. Judy, you need to take some of your

27   life back. Just because you have a baby doesn't mean Judy

28   goes away. You can go to college, you can do whatever you

29   want. You just have to make adjustments.

30   JUDY: I just feel really alone, you know?

31   ANGIE: You kinda are. But roll with it. You're here in this life,

32   make the best of it.

33   JUDY: I guess I am starting to wallow a little in self-pity, huh?

34   ANGIE: A bit.

35   JUDY: Thanks, Angie. You're a good friend.

1   ANGIE: So I'll see you tonight?
2   JUDY: Yeah, you will. *(She gives ANGIE a quick hug.)*
3   ANGIE: And, hey, my sister will be there, too. I'll tell her to
4   bring my niece. Maybe we can set Brian and Tiffany up
5   on a hot date.
6   JUDY: Over this mommy's dead body. My son won't be
7   allowed to date until he's out of high school. God, I just
8   sounded like my mother.
9   ANGIE: Pretty scary. I'll see you later.
10 JUDY: Yeah. Later. *(ANGIE exits. JUDY stands alone for a
11   moment.)* Come on baby Bri. Mommy's got to go to work
12   and then you and I are going to a party.
13
14
15
16
17
18
19
20
21
22
23
24
25
26
27
28
29
30
31
32
33
34
35

Confrontation

(Scene for one man and one woman)

1	*(LEANNA and BRANDON meet, after a long separation, at*
2	*a party.)*
3	**LEANNA:** *(She sits alone, isolating herself from the noise of a*
4	*party in another Off-stage area.)* **Well, this is fun. What**
5	**ever possessed me to come to this party is a mystery to**
6	**me.** *(She pulls a small compact from her purse.)* **So glad I**
7	**took the time to have my roots done so I could impress all**
8	**these people I don't give a** *damn* **about.** *(Yelling)* **I hate**
9	**everyone here!**
10	**BRANDON:** *(He enters on her last line.)* **Oops, sorry...Leanna?**
11	**Is that you?**
12	**LEANNA: Brandon. Of course. Why wouldn't it be you? It's**
13	**been a lousy party, a lousy day, and now, to add insult to**
14	**injury, you come in. Thank you, God. You're a funny guy.**
15	**BRANDON: Ah. Carrying around some unresolved conflicts**
16	**from your past?**
17	**LEANNA: And you're talking to me because...?**
18	**BRANDON: Sorry, I just poked my head in for a minute.**
19	**LEANNA: Well, then, why don't you just poke it back out.**
20	**BRANDON: It's been a long time.**
21	**LEANNA: Not nearly long enough.**
22	**BRANDON: Uh-huh. Well, I'm glad we had this chance to talk,**
23	**to renew old friendships. I'll just be going.**
24	**LEANNA: Go to hell, Brandon.**
25	**BRANDON: Ah, still thinking of opening the Leanna**
26	**MacDonald school of how to win friends and influence**
27	**people?**
28	**LEANNA: Please, sit down, stay a while. I need more crap in**
29	**my life.**
30	**BRANDON: What is with you? This is a party, lots of people**
31	**you haven't seen in a long time, good food, good music,**
32	**nice memories. It's supposed to be a fun thing, you**
33	**know?**
34	**LEANNA: Go to hell, Brandon.**
35	**BRANDON: You are a piece of work, aren't you?**

1   LEANNA: Look who's talking. Why don't you get the hell out

2   of here?

3   BRANDON: You invited me to stay.

4   LEANNA: You can't hear sarcasm?

5   BRANDON: Hey, I just came in to find my fiancée. I can see

6   she's not here, so I'll just be on my way.

7   LEANNA: Your fiancée? You're getting married?

8   BRANDON: That surprises you? I'm over twenty-one.

9   LEANNA: But to make that kind of commitment. To actually

10   be there for someone other than yourself.

11   BRANDON: Listen, you've obviously got some unresolved

12   problems that have nothing to do with me and

13   everything to do with your own screwed-up mind. I

14   haven't seen you in years, I said hello, you said go to hell,

15   I think our conversation has run its course.

16   LEANNA: Witty as you always were. Quite the little

17   wordsmith, aren't you? Of course, I don't remember us

18   doing that much talking lo those many years ago.

19   BRANDON: Jeez, Leanna, that was how long ago?

20   LEANNA: Five years, seven months, two weeks and three

21   days.

22   BRANDON: *(Uncomfortably taken aback)* Oh...I didn't realize...

23   LEANNA: Please, I made that up. It's been about five years. I

24   haven't been counting the days since last we touched,

25   trust me.

26   BRANDON: Oh. I didn't think you had. I mean...never mind.

27   LEANNA: God, there is just no end to your ego, is there? Your

28   name should be Axis, you seem to think the world

29   revolves around you.

30   BRANDON: You seemed to think it did, way back when.

31   LEANNA: Brandon, I was barely fifteen. I was stupid. Only

32   someone as stupid as a fifteen-year-old would get that

33   wrapped up in someone as shallow and superficial as

34   you. Most women grow up and expect to marry a man,

35   not a worm. So did you meet your fiancée on the

1   playground? Still cruising around looking for innocents?

2   BRANDON: I want to know what your problem with me is. We

3   haven't seen each other in years, yet you act like I

4   murdered your family yesterday. So, we made love a long

5   time ago...

6   LEANNA: We didn't make love. I made love, you had sex...

7   BRANDON: OK, it was sex.

8   LEANNA: What surprises me is that I actually thought it was

9   love. It's what you told me.

10   BRANDON: I was a kid myself. I would have said anything to

11   get what I wanted. What are you still so upset about?

12   LEANNA: It meant something to me. It still does.

13   BRANDON: Well, get past it.

14   LEANNA: I can't.

15   BRANDON: What do you want from me? You want me to lie to

16   you and say it meant something special? I was in high

17   school. I'm sorry that you got caught in the fallout.

18   Accept my apologies and move on.

19   LEANNA: That's all it was to you. You are pathetic. You take a

20   little girl and use her. That, no doubt, is what you're

21   going to end up doing to that poor girl you intend on

22   marrying.

23   BRANDON: I love Sarah.

24   LEANNA: You told me you loved me, as I recall.

25   BRANDON: I never told anyone *else* I loved you. Hey, when

26   you're a kid you say what you have to say to get what you

27   want. I'm sorry. What do you want from me?

28   LEANNA: Nothing. You've got nothing to give me that can

29   change anything.

30   BRANDON: If I could take it back, I would. But that was a long

31   time ago.

32   LEANNA: You never even think about it, do you?

33   BRANDON: Honestly? No.

34   LEANNA: Hardly a day goes by that I don't.

35   BRANDON: It wasn't that big a deal, trust me.

1　LEANNA: It was for me. I thought I was someone important
2　　　　to you, that you cared. Obviously I was wrong. People,
3　　　　I've discovered, are only interested in what they want
4　　　　and everyone else be damned. And that is the basic fact
5　　　　of life.
6　BRANDON: *(Beginning to become angry)* No, sweetheart! The
7　　　　basic fact of life is if you don't talk, you can't expect
8　　　　anyone to know what's going on. And here's something
9　　　　else for you to think about. I didn't force you to do
10　　　　anything you didn't want to do. You were a more than
11　　　　willing accomplice, if memory serves.
12　LEANNA: Wrong! I was a child. What you did was practically
13　　　　rape.
14　BRANDON: Take some responsibility for your own actions.
15　　　　You were fifteen, I was seventeen. You could have said no.
16　LEANNA: So could you.
17　BRANDON: Oh, right. You invite me over to your house, your
18　　　　parents are gone for the night, and we end up in your
19　　　　room "watching TV." You know why I didn't call you?
20　　　　Because you were a little too easy. I just wasn't interested
21　　　　in a girl that would be so willing to give herself away.
22　LEANNA: That's a horrible thing to say.
23　BRANDON: Sometimes the truth is pretty ugly. Deal with it
24　　　　and get on with your life.
25　LEANNA: Get on with my life?! You have no idea how hard it
26　　　　has been to just "get on with my life!"
27　BRANDON: It was one time. One crummy time. My God, let
28　　　　it go.
29　LEANNA: That's so easy for you to say.
30　BRANDON: Yeah, it is. Why are you holding on to this? What
31　　　　is the big deal?
32　LEANNA: I got pregnant.
33　BRANDON: *(Pause)* What?
34　LEANNA: That one time, I got pregnant. That's what the big
35　　　　deal is.

1   BRANDON: You got pregnant? How? Never mind, stupid
2   question. Why didn't you tell me?
3   LEANNA: I tried to. You wouldn't listen.
4   BRANDON: When? When did you try?
5   LEANNA: I came over to your house, I looked for you outside
6   the school after your classes, I would wait for you in the
7   parking lot. Hell, I even came to football practice and
8   stood at the sidelines hoping to talk to you.
9   BRANDON: Why didn't you say something?
10   LEANNA: It's hard to talk to the back of a head. You would
11   never look at me. You know as well as I do that you
12   wanted nothing to do with me after you accomplished
13   your goal of bedding me. I was a number to you. Well, my
14   number got called.
15   BRANDON: What happened?
16   LEANNA: Now you're interested?
17   BRANDON: Yes, now I'm interested. I would have been then,
18   too, if you'd given me a chance.
19   LEANNA: Oh no you don't. I tried to talk to you, dammit, I
20   tried.
21   BRANDON: No, you didn't. You would stand there and look at
22   me with those big sad eyes. What the hell was I supposed
23   to do?
24   LEANNA: Oh, I don't know. Maybe show some capacity for
25   human kindness. Ask me what's wrong? I was a kid. I
26   needed you to ask.
27   BRANDON: I was a kid, too. A male kid. You think I needed to
28   have some cow-eyed girl follow me around making me
29   feel guilty for taking her virginity?
30   LEANNA: You could have asked. But you didn't. Completely
31   wrapped up in yourself. But even if you did and I told
32   you, what would you have done?
33   BRANDON: Done?
34   LEANNA: Yeah, done. You know, a course of action, a plan?
35   What would you have done?

1   BRANDON: I don't know.

2   LEANNA: Typical.

3   BRANDON: Dammit, Leanna. You spring this on me years and
4   years after the fact and I'm supposed to come up with
5   instant answers.

6   LEANNA: I knew I wouldn't have been able to count on you.

7   BRANDON: You don't *know* anything. You're speculating.

8   LEANNA: You know I'm right. It would have ended up exactly
9   as it did. I was alone and you went on with your life.

10   BRANDON: Well, it's not like you gave me a chance.

11   LEANNA: I gave you plenty of chances.

12   BRANDON: You never told me!

13   LEANNA: You should have known.

14   BRANDON: I'm sorry, what? I *should* have known? How
15   should I have known?

16   LEANNA: Push comes to shove and the bottom line is you
17   can't count on anyone. You would have left me hanging.

18   BRANDON: Maybe I would have. But we'll never know, will
19   we?

20   LEANNA: I knew then. You would think only of yourself and
21   anyone who got in your way was simply a roadblock to be
22   pushed through. You would have turned your back on
23   me, admit it.

24   BRANDON: Would you have wanted me to marry you? With
25   you at fifteen? And me on my way to college?

26   LEANNA: At least I would have had an option.

27   BRANDON: So would have I, but you took those away. What
28   did you do?

29   LEANNA: What the hell do you think I did? I was alone, I had
30   no choices. I had an abortion.

31   BRANDON: By yourself? You went through that by yourself?

32   LEANNA: Not completely.

33   BRANDON: Did you tell your parents?

34   LEANNA: No. Only one other person knows, the person that
35   took me to have it...taken care of.

1   BRANDON: I should have been that person.
2   LEANNA: You're saying you would have been there for me?
3   Don't make me laugh. I was so low on your list of
4   priorities that I didn't exist.
5   BRANDON: Maybe you're right. Maybe I would have been an
6   ass about it. But you assumed facts not in evidence.
7   LEANNA: Oh, I had plenty of facts. Every time I came up to
8   you, you ran like a rabbit in the other direction.
9   BRANDON: Of course I did. You would come up to me in front
10   of my friends.
11   LEANNA: You were always surrounded by your friends.
12   BRANDON: You could have called me.
13   LEANNA: I tried. But every time I heard the annoyance in
14   your voice when you realized it was me on the line, I
15   knew what you would do.
16   BRANDON: So you would just hang up.
17   LEANNA: I hung up because I was scared. I knew what you
18   would do, and I didn't want to accept it.
19   BRANDON: So you didn't even try?
20   LEANNA: Don't try, don't fail...
21   BRANDON: Good attitude.
22   LEANNA: Being frightened can do that to a person.
23   BRANDON: Why do you think I'm such an ass? You might
24   have been surprised.
25   LEANNA: What would you have done? Married me?
26   BRANDON: No, I wouldn't have married you. But I would
27   have supported you in whatever decision you made.
28   LEANNA: What if I decided to keep it?
29   BRANDON: I can't guess what I would have done. I'd like to
30   say that I would have been a good father and supported
31   you both financially as best I could...
32   LEANNA: But...
33   BRANDON: But I honestly don't know. I was a high school
34   jerk, one of those guys that they write as the fool on TV
35   sitcoms. But I honestly don't think I would have let you

1   go through it alone.

2   LEANNA: It's been my experience that we all end up alone

3   when it comes time to count on someone. You proved

4   that.

5   BRANDON: I proved nothing! I wasn't given a chance to prove

6   myself. You could have tried. So you made all the choices,

7   for me, about me, and without me.

8   LEANNA: Listen, I said what I had to say. I've carried it

9   around for a long time, and now that it's out I guess I can

10   let it go.

11 BRANDON: Yeah, you've carried it around for a long time. You

12   just dumped this on me. I need to deal with it.

13 LEANNA: What's there to deal with? It happened to me, not

14   to you.

15 BRANDON: It happened to both of us. You just didn't bother

16   to share it.

17 LEANNA: I'm going to say this once, OK, and I don't want to

18   go over it again. You made me pregnant when I was

19   fifteen, you ignored me right after it happened, treating

20   me as if I didn't exist. It was a problem I had to deal with

21   in the best way a fifteen-year-old knows how. Maybe I

22   should have had more faith in your nature, but I didn't.

23   But basically, the facts are I carried this anger and

24   hostility around for a long time and directed it at

25   everyone I dealt with and everything I tried. My attitude

26   was that I was alone and you reinforced that, directly or

27   indirectly, it doesn't matter. And, yeah, maybe I should

28   have tried harder to tell you, and maybe, just maybe,

29   you would have been warm and compassionate. I doubt

30   it, but we'll never know. The great thing is, I told you.

31   You wanted me to get past it, to let it go? Well, maybe now

32   I can.

33 BRANDON: So you dump this on me?

34 LEANNA: Dump what? That you impregnated some stupid

35   little girl who had a mad crush on you? I took care of the

1   problem, Brandon. It's done with. And frankly, a day
2   doesn't go by that I don't think about it and have more
3   than a few regrets. But I have to tell you what an ass I
4   always thought you were and finally the reason why. I've
5   waited a long time to do this. God, I feel great.
6   BRANDON: I feel like crap.
7   LEANNA: Then my work here is done.
8   BRANDON: You don't feel the slightest remorse?
9   LEANNA: About the abortion? Yeah. But, from my point of
10   view, I had no choice. I was fifteen and had to make some
11   grown-up choices on my own.
12   BRANDON: What about the way you told me, the way you just
13   screwed up my mind with your news?
14   LEANNA: Hello! This isn't about you. This is about me.
15   BRANDON: You could have counted on me, I'm sure of that.
16   You could have.
17   LEANNA: Well, I'm sure you can't count on anyone except
18   yourself, Brandon. I learned it early and remembered
19   my lesson well.
20   BRANDON: You never gave me an opportunity to prove you
21   wrong.
22   LEANNA: You're a funny guy. It's so easy for you to say this
23   now, from a safe distance from the reality of the
24   situation I actually dealt with. Trust me, you have no
25   idea what you would have done. Or maybe you do...and
26   you can't face the fact of it. Maybe you're not the great
27   compassionate guy you'd like to believe. Think about
28   that one in about fifteen years or so when you and your
29   little wifey have a daughter and she starts dating some
30   cute seventeen-year-old guy who reminds you of yourself.
31   Think about that, my friend. *(She begins to exit.)*
32   BRANDON: I would have helped you to keep the baby.
33   LEANNA: Easy to say now, big guy, when you're already off
34   the hook.
35   BRANDON: I'm not a bad guy.

1   **LEANNA:** **Tell it to someone who cares.** *(She exits.)*
2   **BRANDON:** *(To himself)* **I'm not a bad guy.**
3
4
5
6
7
8
9
10
11
12
13
14
15
16
17
18
19
20
21
22
23
24
25
26
27
28
29
30
31
32
33
34
35

The Waiting Game

(Scene for five men)

1   *(RON, MARK, TODD, DAVID ADAM: All in high school,*
2   *getting ready for a wild weekend together)*
3   **MARK:** *(Enters, looks around, sees he's alone. Dribbles*
4   *basketball for a moment or two. He begins to narrate game.)*
5   **Mark Avery arrives center court. The crowd cheers their**
6   **beloved hero. Mark, humble guy that he is, waves to the**
7   **admiring hordes. The tip off! Mark takes the ball! The**
8   **man is unstoppable! He dodges, he moves, he drives**
9   **down the court. He shoots! It's in! The crowd roars. Mark**
10   **is the king! Mark is the king!** *(He looks over to see RON*
11   *watching him.)* **Hey! Shoot some hoops, loser?**
12   **RON:** Not now, butthead. I've got a date with your mother.
13   **MARK:** Where are the guys?
14   **RON:** I don't know. Adam said he'd be here as soon as he got
15   off work. David had to go to church. *(They both laugh.)*
16   **MARK:** His parents still got him doing that, huh?
17   **RON:** Yep. Some guys never grow up.
18   **MARK:** What about Todd?
19   **TODD:** *(Entering)* What about me? I'm here, got the beer, and
20   you are queer. *(He laughs at his joke.)*
21   **RON:** That's funny. That's what Tiffany said last night about
22   you after your date when she came over to my house for
23   a handful of real man.
24   **TODD:** And that's about all there is...a handful. Where's David?
25   **MARK:** Still off being holy.
26   **TODD:** I can't believe his parents are still making him do this
27   church thing.
28   **RON:** Hey, the guy has no choice. They drive him there, wait
29   till it's over and then take him home. It's not like he can
30   sneak out.
31   **MARK:** Yeah, he has to wait until he's home and his parents
32   are asleep. That's when he can sneak out.
33   **DAVID:** *(Entering on the run)* I made it! Thanks for not leaving
34   without me, guys. I thought my parents would never go
35   to sleep.

1   TODD: I thought you were going to call Adam and he was
2   going to come get you on the corner.
3   DAVID: I waited for him; the jerk never showed up.
4   RON: Well, I don't feel like waiting around forever. He doesn't
5   show up in five minutes, I say we leave without him.
6   MARK: You forget, he's the one with the car.
7   RON: So, we go find him, kick his butt, take his car and head
8   for Palm Springs without him.
9   ADAM: *(Entering)* OK, big man, whose butt is going to get kicked?
10   RON: Yours, you big turd.
11   DAVID: Thanks a lot for coming to get me, pal.
12   MARK: What took you so long?
13   ADAM: Losers. I had to work late. I, unlike you morons,
14   have responsibilities to cover. I have to pay for my car
15   upkeep.
16   RON: Oooohhh, poor baby. You have to put in a few dollars of
17   gas a week.
18   MARK: Correct me if I'm wrong, butthead, but don't Mommy
19   and Daddy pay for insurance, repairs, payments – the
20   list goes on?
21   ADAM: Who do you think has to pay for the gas to keep the
22   Adamobile on the road? And hey, before any of you fools
23   get in my car, I want gas money.
24   TODD: And what's fair about this?! You're the one with the
25   money, why should we have to pay you for gas?
26   ADAM: Because I'm the one with the job.
27   DAVID: Tough job. You go to Daddy's office and turn out the
28   lights and lock up.
29   ADAM: Hey, there's more to it than that. I have to make sure
30   the coffee timer is on too! *(He laughs.)* Pay up, parasites.
31   TODD: I brought the refreshments, I don't have to pay.
32   ADAM: That's fair. *(He turns to the other three.)* Guys? Your
33   coach awaits, but you don't enter until I see the green,
34   green cash of home.
35   MARK: I shouldn't have to pay. This whole thing was my idea.

1   I set everything up. I made the hotel reservation. I made

2   sure that we'd all meet at the appointed time.

3   ADAM: Tough. Pay up.

4   MARK: Who's going to pay my phone bill.

5   ADAM: I care? No. Pay up or no ride.

6   MARK: What a jerk.

7   ADAM: Ron? Cash, please.

8   RON: I shouldn't have to pay. Just the pleasure of my

9   company should be payment enough.

10   TODD: Charge him double.

11   RON: All right, all right.

12   DAVID: *(Reluctantly pulling out his wallet)* It's not fair. You

13   have more money than all of us put together. Why should

14   we have to pay you?

15   ADAM: You know what they say: The rich get richer, the poor

16   get — what was it again, Mark? Is it *children?!*

17   MARK: *(There is a moment of tension.)* I thought I told you not

18   to bring that up, Adam.

19   RON: Lighten up, Mark. It's not like we don't all know about

20   you and Janna.

21   MARK: I told you I don't want to talk about it, OK?

22   DAVID: What?

23   TODD: Mark, my man, you need a beer. Trust me, it will make

24   it all better. It always does.

25   ADAM: I believe that was how he got into the mess originally.

26   DAVID: What mess?

27   MARK: Gimme that beer. *(He downs the whole thing.)* Hey!

28   Let's shoot some hoops for a while. *(He passes the ball to*

29   *RON, who fakes TODD, turns for the shot.)*

30   DAVID: *(Stepping in, grabs the ball.)* What are you guys talking

31   about?

32   ADAM: Well, it seems that young Mr. Avery did the dirty deed

33   with the once-innocent Janna Preston. And, being of

34   unsound mind and even unsounder moral standing,

35   allowed himself to be swayed by something other than

1   common sense, which ultimately resulted in the

2   impending fatherhood he is now waiting to hear about.

3   MARK: *(Trying to change the subject)* I don't know about you

4   guys, but I'm ready to hit the road.

5   RON: And beyond that, our good friend Mark has decided to

6   wait out the answer as far away from the lovely Janna as

7   possible.

8   TODD: He has chosen to spend this time of waiting with us,

9   his lifelong friends.

10   DAVID: And when were you going to tell me? Why am I the

11   last to know?

12   MARK: I didn't realize I had to clear my social calendar with

13   you, Dave. Next time I do the dirty deed, I will give you a

14   call, OK?

15   DAVID: I just think you should've told me, is all.

16   MARK: Are we going or are we staying?

17   RON: I'm ready. I've been ready. Man, I was born ready. Palm

18   Springs, spring break, break-fast, women and me. Ah,

19   free association. My therapist would be so proud.

20   DAVID: Wait a minute. You mean Janna Preston, the

21   sophomore?

22   MARK: David, I said that I was done talking about this, OK?

23   DAVID: It is Janna Preston, the sophomore. I didn't know you

24   were going with her.

25   RON: *(Bursting out with a laugh)* He's not going with her. He

26   *went* with her is about all.

27   ADAM: It's the old story: The popular senior takes advantage

28   of the insecure sophomore yearning for popularity.

29   TODD: *(Jumping into the story)* She sees him from across a

30   crowded room. He waves. "Is that Mark Avery?" she

31   whispers to a friend.

32   RON: *(Taking up the cue)* It's him. It's Mark. *The* Mark Avery.

33   The one and only captain of the football team.

34   ADAM: Senior class vice president.

35   TODD: Mr. B.M.O.C.

1   RON: And he waved at me. *(He swoons.)* **Me!**

2   ADAM: *(Narrating)* **Sensing easy prey, Mark maneuvers over**
3   **to the unsuspecting innocent.**

4   TODD: Hey, baby – he doesn't know her name yet – Hey, baby.

5   RON: *(All aflutter)* Yesss?

6   TODD: You're beautiful, baby. The best-looking chick in the
7   room.

8   RON: *(Batting eyelashes)* Oh, really, do you think so?

9   TODD: Whaddya say we make like a tree and get out of here?

10   RON: Oh, Mark, you're so clever.

11   TODD: *(Putting his arm around RON)* **Come on, baby. I'll take**
12   **you to a real party. By the way, what's your name?** *(TODD,*
13   *ADAM and RON are laughing uproariously at their*
14   *cleverness.)*

15   DAVID: *(Looking at MARK, who is not amused)* **Is that what**
16   **happened?**

17   MARK: Hey, she was cute, I thought she would be fun. I didn't
18   know what would happen. One thing led...

19   DAVID: Yeah, one thing led to another. Janna is my sister's
20   best friend.

21   MARK: Oh?

22   DAVID: I've known her since she was five years old.

23   TODD: Well, I guess Mark knows her a little better than
24   you, huh?

25   DAVID: This isn't funny, guys. I can't believe you are laughing
26   about this.

27   ADAM: Back off, David. You'd be laughing, too, if she was just
28   some girl.

29   TODD: And that's all she is. Some girl.

30   DAVID: She's a friend.

31   RON: No, David, Mr. I-just-got-out-of-church-and-still-have-
32   some-holiness-to-wipe-off-my-shoulders, to Mark at the
33   time she was just another girl willing to pay the price to
34   be with the most popular guy on campus.

35   MARK: I didn't put a gun to her head, you know.

1   DAVID: No, you just took advantage of a situation.
2   MARK: Yeah, well.
3   DAVID: What are you going to do?
4   TODD: Why are you asking him? It's not his problem.
5   MARK: Todd, I'm not a complete jerk. I told her that if she
6   was in trouble, I'd take care of it.
7   RON: You gonna marry her?
8   MARK: *Hell no!* I said I'd take care of it. You know, help her
9   find a doctor in a clinic somewhere, drive her there,
10   make sure she's OK. You know.
11   DAVID: Mark! She's a little girl.
12   ADAM: Not so little as to not get herself in this mess. Hey,
13   David, face it. She took grown-up actions, and now she
14   has to take grown-up responsibilities.
15   MARK: And I said I'd help. For God's sake, I said I'd take care
16   of it. How the hell do you think I feel?
17   DAVID: Maybe you should have thought of this before.
18   RON: Have any of us? I mean, really, have any of us? Think
19   about it, David. When you were going with Julie, did you
20   even think about it? No, you didn't.
21   DAVID: She was on the pill.
22   TODD: That's what she told you. You don't know for sure. It
23   could be you in this situation, you know?
24   ADAM: Just because a girl says she's on the pill, you can never be
25   sure. Ever. Caution, my friends. Caution is what I advise.
26   RON: I have chosen abstinence. *(He raises the glass in a toast to*
27   *himself.)* I am waiting.
28   MARK: Yeah, right, Ron. Waiting. Sure.
29   TODD: You can honestly say that you're going to "wait"?
30   RON: Yep. At least for a while, till I'm old enough to take care
31   of any "problems" that may arise. I look at ole Mark over
32   there and think, there but for the grace of God go any
33   one of us.
34   MARK: *(Seeing them all look at him)* **What are you looking at?**
35   *(They don't answer. They just look.)* **Stop it. Just knock it**

1   off. I don't need your pity. She's probably not even
2   pregnant anyway.
3 ADAM: When do you find out?
4 MARK: Pretty soon. She says she's a little late, but that
5   happens with tension, and stuff, you know.
6 DAVID: And she is pretty young.
7 MARK: Shut up, David, OK? I've heard enough from you.
8 DAVID: Yeah. Great.
9 MARK: Listen, I'm ready to go. I need one night of blind fun.
10   Of not worrying about a future. Of just being with the
11   guys and being a fool.
12 ADAM: And who better than us to provide this. Gentlemen,
13   our chariot awaits.
14 TODD: We need beer.
15 ADAM: No open containers in the car. It's against the law.
16 RON: Hell, Adam, it's against the law for us to even drink.
17   What's wrong with breaking one law and not the other?
18   What an idiot. *(They exit leaving MARK and DAVID On-stage.)*
19 MARK: *(Looking at DAVID)* You comin'?
20 DAVID: You are crazy, just crazy sometimes, you know that,
21   Mark?
22 MARK: *(A little sadly)* Yeah. I know...you comin'?
23 DAVID: Yeah, I'm comin'.
24
25
26
27
28
29
30
31
32
33
34
35

Waiting

(Scene for three women)

1   *(HEATHER and KARA wait with JANNA at the family health*
2   *clinic.)*
3   JANNA: You guys didn't have to come here, you know.
4   HEATHER: Someone should be with you.
5   JANNA: Someone will be with me. Mark said he'd be here.
6   KARA: Uh-huh.
7   JANNA: He did. He said he'd meet me here at two o'clock. He's
8   just a little late.
9   KARA: About an hour. Jan, face it, he's not coming.
10   HEATHER: Shut up for a while, OK, Kara? Don't you see she
11   feels bad enough.
12   KARA: Yeah, I see that. But she needs to face reality. Mark is
13   not coming. We both know that.
14   HEATHER: We don't know it.
15   KARA: Then where is he, huh? Tell me, why are we sitting
16   here with Janna in front of a clinic and Mark is nowhere
17   to be seen? Why is that?
18   JANNA: He's coming. He wouldn't just leave me. He cares
19   about me. He said he loves me.
20   HEATHER: See, Kara? So shut up.
21   KARA: Fine. I'll shut up. We three will just sit out here on the
22   benches until she goes into labor, how's that?
23   HEATHER: What is it, Kara? Is being dumb and awful your
24   hobby? Is it like other people collect stamps? Tell me...
25   JANNA: Both of you, please! That's enough. I'm under enough
26   strain without you two fighting.
27   KARA: Well, whose fault is that? I can't believe you slept with
28   Mark. You're fourteen years old...
29   JANNA: I'm fifteen...
30   KARA: Oh, excuse me. That two days of being fifteen makes
31   all the difference in the world.
32   HEATHER: She's in love. Love makes you do some dumb things.
33   KARA: Yeah, like get pregnant. Pregnant and alone.
34   JANNA: I'm not alone. Mark will be here.
35   HEATHER: And we're here. We won't leave you until Mark

1   gets here.
2 KARA: Then I hope you brought a sleeping bag, 'cause I have
3   a feeling he isn't showing up.
4 HEATHER: Why are you doing this?
5 JANNA: You can be so vicious sometimes, Kara. So mean.
6   You're just jealous because a guy like Mark wants to
7   be with me. Me, a little nobody sophomore, and he's
8   with me.
9 KARA: Is he with you? Well then, look around, Janna. Tell me,
10   where is Mark?
11 HEATHER: You could try to be a little supportive, you know.
12   Mark's a good guy. If he said he would be here, he'll be
13   here. Don't you worry, Jan, you can count on him.
14 KARA: Get real. I've known the guy since I was a kid. He's my
15   brother's best friend. And I know for a fact that he won't
16   be showing up in a while or ever.
17 JANNA: You don't know that. You don't know anything.
18 HEATHER: If Mark said he'd be here, he'll be here. He
19   promised you, didn't he, Janna?
20 KARA: Did he? Did he say he'd be here?
21 JANNA: I told him my appointment was for two-thirty.
22 KARA: It's two forty-five now.
23 JANNA: He's a little late.
24 KARA: But did he actually *say* he'd be here? Or did you just
25   hear what you wanted to hear?
26 JANNA: He'll be here. He wouldn't leave me alone like this. He
27   wouldn't.
28 HEATHER: That's right, he wouldn't. He really cares about
29   you. Mark wouldn't have said he loved you if he didn't
30   mean it.
31 KARA: Am I the only person here with a brain? Am I the only
32   one who sees the difference between reality and fantasy?
33   Because Mark meeting you here today is a fantasy, Jan,
34   face it.
35 HEATHER: You don't know that. Janna, don't pay attention to

1   her. Just because none of her brother's friends would pay

2   any attention to her, she's jealous.

3   KARA: Like I would want one of those losers to come near me.

4   Ron is the only half-way decent guy among them and he's

5   got a girlfriend. The others are just jerks, and Mark is the

6   biggest one. Face it, he used you, abused you, and now

7   he's losing you.

8   JANNA: He's not. He's not!

9   KARA: Yeah, he is. I know for a fact.

10   HEATHER: You don't know anything.

11   KARA: Janna, he's gone.

12   JANNA: Gone? What do you mean?

13   KARA: He went to Palm Springs with all the guys. They left

14   last night. I was hoping he wouldn't go, because I knew

15   you were counting on him, but he went. He went to party

16   and scam, and get together with anyone he can.

17   HEATHER: You don't know that.

18   KARA: Come on, Heather, my brother went with them. Janna,

19   he is not coming today.

20   JANNA: *(Quietly)* Oh, no, no, no. I can't believe he'd do this.

21   KARA: *(Comforting, quietly)* Believe it, honey. He's not going

22   to be here for you today or ever.

23   JANNA: What am I going to do?

24   KARA: What did you think you'd do?

25   JANNA: I don't know. I guess I hoped...well...

26   KARA: What? That he'd marry you? At fifteen years old?

27   HEATHER: But he said he loved her.

28   JANNA: He did. He told me he loved me. People don't say that

29   without meaning it.

30   KARA: Do you know how many girls he's told that to?

31   HEATHER: But this is different. If she's going to have a baby,

32   I mean, that's got to stand for something. It's a bond.

33   JANNA: He'll see that. I mean, if I am pregnant, then we are

34   bonded together in a way that can never be torn apart.

35   HEATHER: He'll want to be with you then. Everything will

1   work out.

2   KARA: How?

3   HEATHER: Well...they'll get married and live with his parents

4   for a while, save their money, then get their own house.

5   He'll get a job and make enough money so you can stay

6   home with the baby. Then after awhile you'll have a little

7   brother or sister. Mark will love you and the kids, and

8   everything will be terrific.

9   JANNA: It will, won't it? His mom and dad like me. And then,

10   when we move out, it will be perfect.

11   HEATHER: And we can have a baby shower for you, and a

12   wedding shower, and a housewarming. With all the

13   presents you get, you won't need anything. You'll see, it

14   will be fine. You are lucky to have someone like Mark.

15   KARA: Hello! We're talking about Mark Avery. The same Mark

16   who scams with as many girls as he can at every stag

17   dance. Do you really think he's going to give that up?

18   JANNA: If we're married he will.

19   KARA: This is not to be believed! Quit reading things into his

20   "I love you." There is nothing in it. He is not going to

21   marry you now or ever. He is just graduating from high

22   school. He's going to college. I can tell you right now, he

23   will not give that up for some little girl in trouble. And do

24   you really believe his parents will welcome you into their

25   home? If Mark marries you, he has to give up college. I'm

26   just sure that having their son married with a pregnant

27   kid for a wife is their idea of heaven. Wake up! Quit being

28   so stupid. Listen to reality!

29   JANNA: *(Quietly, reality setting in)* So, what am I going to do?

30   KARA: You're going to go into the clinic and find out if you're

31   pregnant, that's what. Then we will take it from there.

32   And if you are, then you need to tell your parents right

33   away.

34   JANNA: *No!* I couldn't. There is no way I can tell them this. I

35   can't. They would be so disappointed in me.

1   KARA: Well, they are bound to find out eventually.

2   HEATHER: *(Quietly)* They don't have to. There is an alternative.

3   JANNA: I know. Mark and I talked about it.

4   KARA: Adoption? Your parents would still find out. I mean,
5   unless you came up with some reason to go away until
6   the baby came...oh...you mean...

7   JANNA: Yeah.

8   HEATHER: It's something to think about.

9   KARA: No, it's not.

10   JANNA: Yeah, it is. Kara, you were the one saying I shouldn't
11   have a baby.

12   KARA: No, I said you shouldn't have gotten pregnant. Two
13   different things entirely.

14   JANNA: I realize that. But it is something I have to think
15   about. You're right, of course. There is no way Mark
16   would marry me. I was an idiot to ever think he would.
17   Oh, God, what am I going to do? What am I going to do?
18   Mark isn't coming now, he won't ever be here for me. I
19   am alone.

20   HEATHER: We're here for you.

21   JANNA: Yeah, now. But if I am pregnant, then what? There
22   won't be any wedding shower or housewarming. I know
23   that. I guess I always knew it. And when I'm carrying a
24   baby in my arms, are you going to want to sit with me at
25   a football game? Or help me find a babysitter so I can go
26   to the prom? What have I done? My life is over.

27   HEATHER: You don't have to have a baby.

28   JANNA: I know that. I know.

29   KARA: Abortion just isn't right.

30   JANNA: Neither is being fifteen, pregnant and alone.

31   KARA: So why should a baby pay for your mistakes?

32   HEATHER: Shut up, Kara.

33   KARA: You shut up. You and your talk of marriage and white
34   picket fences. The reality is Janna has a problem and
35   there needs to be more than one way to solve it.

1   JANNA: Bottom line, Kara, it's my choice.

2   KARA: I know that. But you need to look at all the options. Not

3   just take the fast and easy way out.

4   JANNA: This is my life we're talking about. My life. And my

5   life is over if I don't figure out what to do. My entire life

6   will be messed up for good. And Mark will just go on, no

7   problems. What have I done? I am in so much trouble.

8   HEATHER: And he walks away clean.

9   JANNA: What am I going to do?

10   KARA: Janna, calm down. We're here for you now, that's what

11   counts. Let's go into the clinic and find out if you're

12   pregnant or not. Maybe there's nothing to worry about at

13   all. You could just be late.

14   HEATHER: Yeah, that's probably all it is. You're just late.

15   JANNA: I'm never late. I'm so messed up.

16   HEATHER: Come on. Let's go in and see what happens. I

17   guarantee everything will be OK. It will be fine.

18   JANNA: You really think so?

19   HEATHER: Yeah, I do. It will be fine.

20   JANNA: OK. You guys wait out here, OK? I need to do this

21   alone. *(She exits.)*

22   HEATHER: Are you sure Mark went to Palm Springs?

23   KARA: Yeah.

24   HEATHER: What a complete ass.

25   KARA: Yeah, I know.

26   HEATHER: That could be me in her position right now, you

27   know? I fell for Mark's lines, too.

28   KARA: I know.

29   HEATHER: How? How do you know?

30   KARA: My brother David tells me about all the girls Mark gets

31   together with.

32   HEATHER: How does he know?

33   KARA: Mark tells everyone.

34   HEATHER: Oh, damn.

35   KARA: Yeah.

1   HEATHER: He actually told me he loved me.

2   KARA: Did he? Are you sure?

3   HEATHER: What do you mean, am I sure?

4   KARA: Mark makes it a point to never say "I love you" to

5   anyone.

6   HEATHER: But he did...

7   KARA: Think about it. Didn't he say something like, "I love

8   how you..." and then fill in the blank? I love how you

9   laugh, I love the way you think, I love your personality, I

10   love...

11   HEATHER: But...

12   KARA: You heard what you wanted to hear. You wanted a guy

13   like Mark to think you were special. He doesn't. You were

14   just one more on a very long list. You just didn't get

15   caught. Unfortunately, Janna was not as lucky.

16   HEATHER: There but for the grace of God...

17   KARA: Yeah. *(A pause)* What do you think she's going to do?

18   HEATHER: What would you do?

19   KARA: I don't know. I really don't know.

20   HEATHER: I bet she doesn't either.

21   KARA: *(Softly, a deep breath, looking off after JANNA)* **Damn.**

22

23

24

25

26

27

28

29

30

31

32

33

34

35

Beginning to the End

(Scene for one man and one woman)

1   *(SHE and HE go through their relationship from when it*
2   *starts to the final moment. Note: They do not speak directly*
3   *to each other until specified in the script.)*

4   SHE: We've been seeing each other for a while now.

5   HE: I asked her to go out with me about a month ago.

6   SHE: He's the cutest guy I've ever known.

7   HE: She's perfect. There's nothing I would change about her.

8   SHE: He's the nicest guy. So sweet.

9   HE: She's so nice. My parents love her.

10   SHE: My parents love him.

11   HE: She's the best thing that ever happened to me.

12   SHE: I know that our relationship will grow and grow and
13   only get better.

14   HE: She's the best thing that ever happened to me.

15   SHE: We never fight.

16   HE: We hardly ever disagree.

17   SHE: We feel the same about almost everything.

18   HE: It's like we think the same thoughts.

19   SHE: Well, we do have one disagreement.

20   HE: There is one thing that kind of hangs us up.

21   SHE: It's not that he doesn't love me.

22   HE: I don't know what the problem is. I love her. She knows
23   that.

24   SHE: I know he loves me. He says he does. He wouldn't lie
25   about that.

26   HE: I respect her, I love her, everything. I don't know how else
27   I can make her believe me. I would never hurt her.

28   SHE: I want to prove to him that I believe him and that I love
29   him. It's just that...

30   HE: I don't know what the big deal is. I mean, I know we'll
31   end up married some day. I feel it in my heart. There's no
32   one else for me but her.

33   SHE: I feel like I'm disappointing him by holding back. But if
34   I don't, that means I give up everything to him. Not that
35   I don't want to. I do. But I don't know if I'm ready now.

1   Not yet.
2   HE: I know that I'm ready. I think she is, too, but I think she's
3   got some "social hang-up" about it. Like she's worried
4   about what people will think. She should only be
5   concerned about us, not anyone else. It's us that's
6   important.
7   SHE: He is the most important thing to me. Maybe I'm just
8   being silly.
9   HE: Not that I'd break up with her over this, but it's
10   frustrating.
11   SHE: I just love him so much. I do. Maybe saying it isn't
12   enough.
13   HE: She called me and said she wanted to see me.
14   SHE: I've thought a lot about it.
15   HE: She said it was important.
16   SHE: So, I made up my mind.
17   HE: She said it would be something special.
18   SHE: I want it to be special.
19   HE: I wonder...I hope...
20   SHE: I hope he will always love me.
21   HE: She's the best thing that ever happened to me.
22   SHE: Words just aren't enough.
23   HE: I know that I will be with her forever. Especially now.
24   SHE: I never knew I could feel so loved.
25   HE: I love her. She must know that. We are as close as two
26   people can be.
27   SHE: We share such a special experience. No one else will
28   ever have that part of my soul. I feel like I could fly.
29   HE: I feel like I am floating. Nothing will ever compare to how
30   I feel right now.
31   SHE: My heart is wide open, and he is there, inside of me,
32   taking all of me, being a part of me.
33   HE: This is what love is. I would do anything for her.
34   SHE: He walks into the room and my heart skips a beat. He
35   fills the room with his light.

1   HE: She is like the sun and the moon and the stars all in one.

2   SHE: I will never feel like this with anyone else. This is it, he

3   is all that there is.

4   HE: Forever.

5   SHE: I feel so different.

6   HE: Things will always be like this between us.

7   SHE: I feel different.

8   HE: Things will never change.

9   SHE: Things aren't right.

10   HE: She's been acting kinda funny lately.

11   SHE: I don't feel too good.

12   HE: She's so moody.

13   SHE: I feel like crap.

14   HE: What's her problem? Everyday she's in a mood. It's

15   getting old.

16   SHE: Something's just not right. Not with me, not with us.

17   HE: I'm getting really tired of her attitude lately.

18   SHE: I've been so moody lately. I don't know what's wrong.

19   HE: Things are still good, you know, between us. But other

20   stuff, just talking and all, that's not so good. It's like we

21   have nothing to say to each other without it turning into

22   a disagreement. Not really a fight, but bickering. And it's

23   not my fault. It's her.

24   SHE: He picks on me. No matter what I do or say, he has to

25   comment on it. And I'm crying all the time lately. And

26   when I cry I get "nerve-hungry" so I have to eat. I've

27   probably gained five pounds.

28   HE: I don't know what her problem is, but it better stop. At

29   first the tears were kind of cute, but now it's just old.

30   SHE: I'm tired of crying.

31   HE: She better snap out of it.

32   SHE: I'm so tired all the time.

33   HE: She's getting to be such a drag to be around. She's

34   always tired.

35   SHE: Maybe I need vitamins or something.

1   HE: Something's up with her.
2   SHE: It's not vitamins I need.
3   HE: She said she needs to be alone for a couple days.
4   SHE: I need to think things through.
5   HE: Alone. Alone alone, not together alone. I can feel that
6   things are not right.
7   SHE: I can't shut him out now. I need him.
8   HE: She's shutting me out. Maybe she's found someone else.
9   SHE: I need him to be there.
10 HE: If she's tired of me, fine. Hey, whatever.
11 SHE: I'm going to tell him today.
12 HE: She said she wanted to see me today. I wonder if this is it.
13   The end. After the way she's been for the last few weeks,
14   that would be fine with me. I don't need the moods.
15 SHE: I need for him to be strong. To be understanding and
16   loving.
17 HE: I need her to lighten up.
18 SHE: I don't know how I'm going to say this.
19 HE: I'm tired of the whining.
20 SHE: I need to talk to him soon.
21 HE: She called me last night to ask me to meet her before
22   school starts. I guess that means we're cutting morning
23   classes. Hmmm. This doesn't sound good.
24 SHE: I asked him to meet me before school, that way we could
25   skip classes and be alone.
26 HE: I don't like cutting classes. Not when we're this close to
27   graduation and I have a good chance at a scholarship.
28   This better be important.
29 SHE: Some things are just more important than school right
30   now, you know?
31 HE: She says she "needs to talk." That can only mean trouble.
32 SHE: I need to talk to him. It's serious, you know...
33 HE: I know this is going to be something serious. Some really
34   serious stuff.
35 SHE: I'm worried how he'll take this.

1   HE: I mean, what's the worst it could be?
2   SHE: This is the worst thing that could happen. I thought we
3   were so careful.
4   HE: She's pregnant. Pregnant.
5   SHE: I'm pregnant.
6   HE: What a weird word. Say it out loud. Pregnant. It's not a
7   word that is easy to say.
8   SHE: Pregnant. Try saying it fast five times without gagging. I
9   guess it's not so hard when you're not the one who's in
10   the condition.
11   HE: What does she want from me?
12   SHE: What are we going to do?
13   HE: She said she was on the pill.
14   SHE: I started the pill. But I guess I was too late or missed a
15   day or something. I never needed it before because I
16   never did this with anyone before.
17   HE: She told me there wouldn't be a problem.
18   SHE: I didn't think that this could happen to someone
19   like me.
20   HE: I can't believe this is happening.
21   SHE: I'm so scared.
22   HE: My life is shot to hell.
23   SHE: What am I going to do?
24   HE: She's so irresponsible.
25   SHE: He's so angry.
26   HE: I feel like I've been betrayed.
27   SHE: The look in his eyes. I will never forget that look.
28   HE: OK, think. What am I going to do?
29   SHE: It's not like I planned for this to happen.
30   HE: This was definitely not in my plans.
31   SHE: He just looked at me and walked away.
32   HE: I didn't know what to say to her. I still don't.
33   SHE: He walked away.
34   HE: I just walked away. I mean, I'm going to call her and talk
35   about what she is...we are going to do.

1   SHE: He called me last night. He sounded so distant.

2   HE: I could hardly talk to her. I'm so mad.

3   SHE: I didn't do this alone, you know.

4   HE: This is so wrong. I have plans. I'm going to college, I got a

5   great scholarship.

6   SHE: He acts like he's the only one who's affected by this.

7   HE: I can't just give it all up.

8   SHE: This is my life.

9   HE: She can't expect me to give everything up.

10   SHE: I'll have to give everything up.

11   HE: I won't be an adult when I haven't had time to be a kid.

12   SHE: I'm so scared.

13   HE: Why did this happen?

14   SHE: What if he never calls me again?

15   HE: I have to call her and get this settled.

16   SHE: He said he loved me. Was that a lie?

17   HE: I do love her. But, I mean, maybe she's not the right one.

18   SHE: He told me that he'd always be there for me. Always. I

19   thought he was the right one.

20   HE: I guess I was wrong.

21   SHE: What am I going to do?

22   HE: What does she want me to do?

23   SHE: Will I have to quit school?

24   HE: I'll have to give up college and get a job.

25   SHE: College is out.

26   HE: I'll probably have to marry her.

27   SHE: How can I have a career and a baby?

28   HE: I could join the army, I guess. That way I'd get paid and

29   could save for college.

30   SHE: I don't want to do this.

31   HE: My parents are going to flip out...

32   SHE: I can't have a baby.

33   HE: ...but, maybe if I tell them about it in a way that shows

34   them I'm handling it. Show them that I can take care of

35   things.

1   SHE: I don't want a baby, Not now.

2   HE: It could work out.

3   SHE: He doesn't want it either. Look how he acted.

4   HE: I'll call her tonight.

5   SHE: I am totally alone in this.

6   HE: Maybe she'll go away and have the baby and then we can
7   figure something out.

8   SHE: I am on my own. He's made that crystal clear.

9   HE: She wasn't home. Her mom said she was over at Angela's
10   house spending the night. But I went over there and no
11   one answered the door.

12 SHE: I need to think this through.

13 HE: I'll see her at school later. Tell her that, even though I am
14   not happy about all this, I will take care of my
15   responsibility.

16 SHE: It's my responsibility. It's my body.

17 HE: She wasn't at school and when I called her at home, no
18   one answered. What is going on?

19 SHE: I feel like I'm dying inside.

20 HE: Where is she?

21 SHE: I made an appointment for the clinic for this afternoon.
22   Angela said she'd go with me. I suppose I should tell him,
23   but why?

24 HE: What is she doing?

25 SHE: When I first told him what was going on and he walked
26   away, he walked out on me, on the situation, on
27   everything I ever put my trust in.

28 HE: Angela told me that she was going to the clinic with her.

29 SHE: I can never trust him again.

30 HE: She can't do this.

31 SHE: *(She faces him.)* It's my life.

32 HE: *(He faces her.)* It's my baby, too.

33 SHE: You should have thought of that before you walked away.

34 HE: What did you expect me to do? I was shocked. It wasn't
35   what I expected.

1   SHE: Funny, I said the same thing to myself as I watched you
2   leave.
3   HE: You can't do this.
4   SHE: Try and stop me.
5   HE: But I love you.
6   SHE: Well, you have a helluva way of showing it.
7   HE: If you're doing this to punish me, it's the wrong way. I
8   don't want you to do this.
9   SHE: Oh, really? So, you're ready to give up college, get
10   married, pay bills, have a mortgage, and create a world
11   for a child to live in? You're ready for all that, huh?
12   HE: No, I'm not ready. But there's really not much choice
13   now, is there?
14   SHE: *(Quietly)* Yes, there is a choice. And it's my choice.
15   HE: Don't do this.
16   SHE: I have to.
17   HE: I told you, things will work out.
18   SHE: How? You join the army, travel around, save money, you
19   go to college, you have your life. While I stay home and
20   have the baby and find out in ten years that you don't love
21   me enough to stay with me or the child after all? I'll be
22   under thirty, with a ten-year-old and no future. Is that
23   your plan for me?
24   HE: How can you say that? I love you. You know I do.
25   SHE: I thought you did. But you loved a little girl who thought
26   the sun rose and set on you. Well, in the last few weeks
27   I've had to grow up and make some hard choices.
28   HE: What about my choices?
29   SHE: You have none.
30   HE: I can't believe you would do this.
31   SHE: I can't either. But I am. And I will have to live with it.
32   HE: We're through, then, if you do this.
33   SHE: *(A long look)* We were through anyway.
34   HE: At least let me go in with you. We can talk to someone, a
35   counselor. There are other options.

1 SHE: I've talked to the counselor. I am being set up with a
2   good family.
3 HE: What?
4 SHE: I'm meeting with the family today that will adopt the
5   baby.
6 HE: Adopt? You mean you're not having an abortion?
7 SHE: An abortion? No! How could you think I would do that?
8 HE: But...I just assumed.
9 SHE: How could you think that? Don't you know me at all?
10 HE: I guess I just thought that...
11 SHE: Thought what? After all this time we've been together,
12   you actually believed that I could have an abortion?
13 HE: I'm sorry, I...
14 SHE: Go away, please.
15 HE: No. I need to be a part of this.
16 SHE: Why?
17 HE: I don't know. I just do.
18 SHE: This is my decision, you know. You have no choices
19   in this.
20 HE: I know.
21 SHE: Then why do you want to be there?
22 HE: I just want to be.
23 SHE: OK. *(He starts to put his hand on her back to guide her in.*
24   *She quietly responds to his touch without anger, just very*
25   *matter of fact.)* Don't touch me.
26 HE: Sorry. *(They exit.)*
27
28
29
30
31
32
33
34
35

Perspectives on
CONTROL

Power Trip

Out of Control

Part of the Crowd

Power Trip

(Scene for one man and one woman)

1   *(ALICE and MATT are On-stage from the start. However, the*
2   *scene opens with what appears to be a bare stage, except for*
3   *the presence of a single couch. After a moment or so, we*
4   *hear a noise, then)*
5   **ALICE Matt, come on.**
6   **MATT: What?**
7   **ALICE: Be nice.**
8   **MATT: I'm trying to be nice. I want to be really nice. Don't you**
9   **want to be nice with me?**
10 **ALICE: Matt.** *(A slight giggle)*
11 **MATT: Oh, Alice, Alice, take me to Wonderland...**
12 **ALICE: Now, stop. I mean it.** *(A silence again, then)* **Matt!**
13 **MATT: What?** *(His head pops up.)* **What?**
14 **ALICE: I'm serious. Really.** *(Her head pops up.)* **I am.**
15 **MATT: OK. Fine.**
16 **ALICE: Oh, now you're mad?**
17 **MATT: No.**
18 **ALICE: Yes you are.** *(She gets playful.)* **Tell Mama all about it.**
19   **Why is my baby mad?**
20 **MATT: I'm not mad.**
21 **ALICE: Then come here.** *(She puts her arm around him and*
22   *they both disappear again.)*
23 **MATT: You make me crazy, Alice, you really do.**
24 **ALICE: Good.** *(Again a small silence)* **Matt! I told you not to do**
25   **that!**
26 **MATT:** *(Up)* **What do you want from me? What is this game**
27   **you're playing?**
28 **ALICE: I'm not playing any games.**
29 **MATT: Oh, no? You are the biggest tease.**
30 **ALICE: Tease? Why? Because I won't give in to your demands?**
31 **MATT: What demands? Have I demanded anything from you?**
32 **ALICE: Not in so many words. But this little emotional power**
33   **trip you go on every time we're together is getting a little**
34   **old.**
35 **MATT: Me making a power trip? Who has been saying "yes"**

1 with one breath then "no" with the next?
2 ALICE: I shouldn't even have to say no to you. You should
3   know it instinctively. You know exactly how far I will go.
4   We've talked about it many times.
5 MATT: Talk. That's all we do is talk. We've talked the subject
6   right into the ground. Don't you think it's time we moved
7   this relationship forward?
8 ALICE: Excuse me?
9 MATT: Made progress, move to a new level of understanding.
10 ALICE: Explain "new level of understanding."
11 MATT: Either a relationship grows or it stagnates.
12 ALICE: Stagnates?
13 MATT: Yes. It sits and festers and smells and goes nowhere,
14   just like we are now. Going nowhere, day after day, the
15   same old thing. We need to experience new plateaus or
16   what's the point of being together?
17 ALICE: Caring about each other isn't enough?
18 MATT: Caring is good. Caring is a very good thing. But we've
19   done caring. It's time to do more.
20 ALICE: More than just caring. I see. So what you are saying is
21   that our relationship, what we have together and built
22   over time is fast becoming a scum-filled pond, a breeding
23   ground for disease and despair?
24 MATT: Yes! That's the perfect description of what we have
25   here by not moving ahead.
26 ALICE: OK, where is it?
27 MATT: Where is what?
28 ALICE: The camera. This has to be some sort of setup for one
29   of those tacky white trash afternoon talk shows. There is
30   no way on this earth that you would spout that kind of
31   weak-minded line without prompting from Ricki Lake or
32   Sally Jesse Raphael.
33 MATT: I'm serious. We have obviously reached a point in this
34   alliance where we have to make some sort of decision.
35 ALICE: Alliance? What are we now? NAFTA? Are we creating

1 some sort of trade agreement? I give you access to my
2 northern region and you allow me the rights to your
3 letterman's jacket?
4 MATT: Now you're being ridiculous
5 ALICE: I'm being ridiculous? You tell me that if we don't get
6 more intimate physically then we have no relationship?
7 MATT: That's not what I'm saying.
8 ALICE: Then what are you saying?
9 MATT: You know, if you really had any true feelings for me...
10 ALICE: Don't go there, Matt.
11 MATT: Don't go where?
12 ALICE: The "if you really loved me" routine.
13 MATT: I wasn't going to say that. *(She gives him a dubious*
14 *look.)* I wasn't...but now that you bring it up.
15 ALICE: I'm outta here.
16 MATT: No, wait. God, you just get me so confused.
17 ALICE: Not hard to do when you are not thinking with your
18 brains.
19 MATT: You know, you don't make this any easier. It's much
20 more difficult for guys than it is for girls.
21 ALICE: Is it?
22 MATT: Yeah. I mean, you can turn it on and turn it off
23 anytime. It's like this little faucet of power for women to
24 play with men's minds, get them all turned around and
25 upset, then they flounce out, morals held high while the
26 guy ends up feeling like a dirty pig.
27 ALICE: *(In complete disbelief)* What?
28 MATT: It's true. Women do that kind of stuff all the time.
29 ALICE: Do we? Do we really?
30 MATT: Don't act like you don't know what I'm talking about.
31 You women have these little codes between you, like
32 some little club that they keep men out of so the women
33 are in total control of the situation.
34 ALICE: I don't have a clue what you are talking about.
35 MATT: Look at women. Look at their bodies and how they

106

1   move. How is any man supposed to keep control? And
2   women know this. You probably all talk about it during
3   your little meetings in the bathrooms. Don't think we
4   men don't notice how you can never seem to go to a
5   bathroom alone. Always in pairs, or in groups. It's
6   probably where all the planning is done. Little confabs
7   by the stalls. Exchanging female information in front of
8   the hand dryers.
9   ALICE: You seem to have this all figured out.
10 MATT: I think about it a lot.
11 ALICE: That would explain your grades.
12 MATT: There is a great chasm of difference between men and
13   women. We look at sex from very different viewpoints.
14   You need to think about it.
15 ALICE: Oh, I have. However, I haven't given it nearly as much
16   focus in my life as you so obviously have.
17 MATT: You don't think about it like a man does.
18 ALICE: Not to the point of obsession. You are borderline on
19   this one.
20 MATT: Listen to what I'm saying. Sit down and listen.
21 ALICE: Illuminate me on the great differences between men
22   and women.
23 MATT: The way I see it is that men are stronger...
24 ALICE: Hey...
25 MATT: Physically! I mean physically. Which is my point
26   exactly. See, women are weak.
27 ALICE: Hey, again!
28 MATT: But they are, at least most of them. So there is this
29   constant struggle for superiority between the sexes. Men
30   are physically more capable. Grant me that one, OK?
31 ALICE: On balance, yes, that is one I will give you.
32 MATT: But emotionally and mentally, women are stronger...
33 ALICE: Now you're making sense.
34 MATT: Aha! So you see, men are focused on the physical.
35 ALICE: Well, you're a perfect example of that.

1   MATT: Yes, I am, as you are the perfect example of the
2   prehistoric emotionally charged woman.
3   ALICE: *(Dubious)* Uh-huh.
4   MATT: It all dates back to ancient times when the men would
5   go out and hunt while the women would stay and take
6   care of whatever the man brought back to the cave. Ever
7   since that time there has been a conflict between men
8   and women for power. Men use their strength to prove
9   themselves, women use their abilities to please the man
10   by doing for him.
11 ALICE: Doing for him. Uh-huh. Go on.
12 MATT: See, men are physically tough, hard. Women, on the
13   other hand, are soft and pliable. But mentally, it's
14   opposite. Women, in order to fulfill the needs of the man,
15   must be strong. On the other hand, while the man,
16   exhausted from his days spent in the fields of labor and
17   combat, needs to be mentally massaged, physically
18   content, in order for him to continue the species.
19 ALICE: So what you are saying here is that you have some
20   primal physical needs that I, through some sort of
21   evolutionary expedience and subconscious need, want to
22   satisfy.
23 MATT: Exactly! That's it exactly!
24 ALICE: And by satisfying this primitive need in you I will, in
25   turn, be making myself feel more powerful.
26 MATT: Yes! That's it!
27 ALICE: Do you think I'm the dumbest person in this country,
28   or just this state?
29 MATT: Huh?
30 ALICE: Did you just make that up as you went along or did
31   you actually put in some effort on your own time coming
32   up with this pile of nonsense?
33 MATT: Not buying it, huh?
34 ALICE: Not hardly.
35 MATT: You gotta admit, it was pretty good, though.

1   ALICE: You're crazy.
2   MATT: Just about you. And I want to communicate my
3   feelings for you in the most intimate way I know how.
4   This next step would simply be a physical expression of
5   my respect and love.
6   ALICE: You are so pathetic.
7   MATT: Not buying that, either, huh?
8   ALICE: Nope.
9   MATT: I don't know what you want from me anymore. You
10   know, I try to be considerate of your feelings about this
11   whole thing, but you have no consideration of my
12   feelings. Why is it you're the one who sets the
13   boundaries, who says "yes" or "no"?
14 ALICE: Because it's my body.
15 MATT: I have a body, too, you know.
16 ALICE: And you can do whatever you want with it...
17 MATT: I'm trying to...
18 ALICE: As long as it doesn't interfere with what I'm doing...
19 MATT: Or not doing...
20 ALICE: Or not doing with mine.
21 MATT: This is getting us nowhere.
22 ALICE: It's the same old argument we always have. I say no,
23   you get mad, or hurt, or stupid, I leave, you call me the
24   next day and apologize and we get back together. Why
25   don't we skip all the stupid stuff and just get back
26   together?
27 MATT: There you go again. This is all just some sort of strange
28   and bizarre power trip for you, isn't it?
29 ALICE: I beg your pardon.
30 MATT: A power trip. You just laid out exactly what we go
31   through, and you're right. And I do get upset, and you do
32   leave and I do come crawling back to you like some little
33   worm-like creature with no backbone or pride.
34 ALICE: So what are you saying?
35 MATT: I'm saying that this is getting a little old. I don't know

1   if I want to do it anymore.

2   ALICE: Because I won't give in to you, you want to break up.

3   MATT: I don't know. Maybe. Yeah, maybe I do. How do you
4   feel about that?

5   ALICE: *(Gives him a long look.)* OK.

6   MATT: OK?

7   ALICE: OK.

8   MATT: OK, what?

9   ALICE: We won't do this anymore.

10   MATT: We won't?

11   ALICE: Not if it makes you this unhappy.

12   MATT: So we're breaking up? You can make that kind of
13   decision that fast?

14   ALICE: I didn't say we were breaking up.

15   MATT: But you said we won't do this... *(The light dawns!)* Oh!

16   ALICE: You want it? Here it is, come and get it.

17   MATT: You're serious.

18   ALICE: I've never been more serious in my life. *(She begins to*
19   *unbutton her top.)*

20   MATT: Omigod. You are serious.

21   ALICE: Yes. That's how much you mean to me. I don't want to
22   lose you.

23   MATT: *(Holding her)* Oh, Alice. You won't regret this.

24   ALICE: Maybe, maybe not. I hope you enjoy yourself.

25   MATT: I will. We both will. *(He tries to kiss and nuzzle her; she*
26   *is unresponsive.)* You want to, you know, move a little?
27   Kinda help me out?

28   ALICE: I said come and get it. I didn't say I would cooperate.

29   MATT: What?

30   ALICE: Well, Matt, having access to my body obviously means
31   a lot to you. Much more than my feelings mean. So, you
32   go ahead and help yourself. *(She holds her arms out to her*
33   *sides.)* Go on. Do whatever it is you need to do.

34   MATT: You think I won't, huh? You think you can screw with
35   my mind and I will just collapse into this mush man.

1   Well, you are wrong, missy. Watch my smoke.

2   ALICE: Fine. *(She stares over his shoulder, expressionless,*

3   *yawns.)* You need help with that snap?

4   MATT: *Dammit!* You...! I...! This is just...! I want...! I mean...!

5   Forget it.

6   ALICE: What?

7   MATT: You heard what I said, forget it.

8   ALICE: Why? Isn't this what you want? Here I am. Waiting to

9   please my man just like my prehistoric sisters did many

10   eons ago.

11   MATT: You're good. You know that? You're really, really good.

12   ALICE: Yeah. I am.

13   MATT: You knew I wouldn't go through with it, didn't you?

14   ALICE: Yeah.

15   MATT: See, you win again. These little power struggles, these

16   little mind games of control, I always lose.

17   ALICE: This isn't a game, Matt. This is life. These are choices

18   I am making that have nothing to do with you.

19   MATT: Well, thanks so much.

20   ALICE: But they don't. You think I'm made of stone? Well, I'm

21   not. But Matt, I will be damned if I will give myself to you

22   just to keep us together.

23   MATT: But I would.

24   ALICE: That's you and your choice. However, my choice is to

25   not do that. And Matt, if this is really such a difficult

26   thing for you, then you need to find someone else to be

27   with, because I am not changing who I am or what I

28   believe just to make you happy.

29   MATT: Yeah, I know. Dammit, I know.

30   ALICE: You say that this is a power struggle. Well, maybe it is.

31   But my power struggle is with me. I look at your

32   beautiful face, those big brown eyes, and those terrific

33   shoulders and, trust me, I am having just as hard a time

34   of keeping myself under control as you are.

35   MATT: But look. See how weak I am? You still respect me and

1   care about me, even though I'm weak and so helpless
2   about giving in to my base desires.
3 ALICE: Of course I still respect and care about you, even
4   though you are a sniveling, whining weak-minded man.
5 MATT: And I'd still respect and care about you if you gave in
6   to your desires. Even more, because it would mean we
7   have just that much more in common. See?
8 ALICE: You are so pathetic.
9 MATT: Be pathetic with me.
10 ALICE: Don't whine, Matt.
11 MATT: So, this is it, huh?
12 ALICE: Yep.
13 MATT: Forever?
14 ALICE: For as long as I can see into the foreseeable future. At
15   least until there is a ring on this finger.
16 MATT: I'll go to K-Mart and buy you a ring tomorrow.
17 ALICE: You know what I mean.
18 MATT: Yeah, I do. And I do respect you for it. I don't like it, but
19   I do respect you in some sort of wimpy, unmasculine part
20   of me.
21 ALICE: Well, thank you. Come here and kiss me, you silly
22   thing.
23 MATT: *(Like it's a chore.)* OK, if I have to.
24 ALICE: You don't have to do anything you don't want to.
25 MATT: I'll make the sacrifice. Maybe you can learn from my
26   example.
27 ALICE: Just shut up and come here. *(They disappear behind*
28   *the couch again. A moment of silence)* **Matt!**
29 MATT: Sorry, sorry, sorry, sorry.
30
31
32
33
34
35

Out of Control

(Scene for one man and one woman)

1   *(BILL and MARY give their points of view about their*
2   *breakup. Note: All "..." mean the characters pick up the line*
3   *before the end of the preceding sentence.)*
4   **BILL and MARY: There was nothing I could do. You don't**
5   **understand. You weren't there.**
6   **MARY: He was out of control...**
7   **BILL: She was out of control...**
8   **MARY: He was like a crazy man. I was truly frightened...**
9   **BILL: Frightening. That's the only word I can think of. She**
10   **came at me like a crazy woman...**
11   **MARY: The guy is crazy.**
12   **BILL: I just went to see how she was; I was concerned. Hey, we**
13   **were together for a long time. It's natural...**
14   **MARY: It's unnatural. He was checking up on me. He always**
15   **did. He never trusted me. That's why I broke it off with**
16   **him...**
17   **BILL: I broke it off with her. She said she couldn't trust me. I**
18   **don't know where that came from. But I wanted to make**
19   **sure she was OK.**
20   **MARY: He was OK at first. Then, jeez, all hell broke loose. He**
21   **came over about ten o'clock that morning...**
22   **BILL: I went over about ten o'clock that morning. She was**
23   **alone...**
24   **MARY: I was alone.**
25   **BILL and MARY: That made me a little nervous...**
26   **MARY: Being alone with him, I mean...**
27   **BILL: I mean, I never knew what to expect...**
28   **MARY: The whole thing was completely unexpected...**
29   **BILL: I just wanted to see how she was...**
30   **MARY: I was sitting on the chair, reading a book and there**
31   **was a knock at the door.** *(Her version of the scene begins.)*
32   **BILL: Anybody home?**
33   **MARY:** *(Quietly)* **Oh, shit.** *(Out loud)* **Just a minute.** *(She lets*
34   *him in.)* **Hey, how you doin'?**
35   **BILL: Are you alone?**

1   MARY: Uh. Yeah. But my parents will be back soon.

2   BILL: Oh, yeah? I heard they were on vacation in Mexico.

3   MARY: Oh. Yeah, well, they might be coming home early.

4   BILL: Uh-huh. So, can I sit?

5   MARY: Sure. I guess. Really, though, you can't stay long.

6   BILL: No?

7   MARY: No. See, I really shouldn't have anyone here without
8   my parents being home. So...

9   BILL: So? I have to leave soon? Is that what you're saying?

10 MARY: Well, yes, I guess it is.

11 BILL: Are you expecting someone else?

12 MARY: No, I'm not.

13 BILL: So you're here. Alone. Not waiting for anyone?

14 MARY: Please leave.

15 BILL: Since when do you tell me when to come and when to go?

16 MARY: Bill, I think you should leave now.

17 BILL: Do you? Do you really?

18 MARY: Come on, Bill. Just go.

19 BILL: I'll go when I'm ready. And I'm not ready. So watch your
20   mouth. Don't tell me what to do. I never liked when you
21   told me what to do. Never. Or don't you remember that?

22 MARY: I know, Bill.

23 BILL: I don't think you do. Maybe you need a little reminder,
24   huh? *(He crosses to her threateningly, then freezes.)*

25 MARY: *(Coming out of the scene)* It was always like that. He
26   was always trying to control me, threatening me,
27   grabbing me. *(She moves back into the scene.)*

28 BILL: *(Coming out of the scene)* She had called me a couple
29   days before and sounded down, so I just wanted to say hi.
30   I mean, I'm not a complete ass. I was concerned. So I
31   went over there. She seemed happy to see me at first. *(He
32   moves back into the scene.)*

33 MARY: *(Hugging him)* Bill. Hi.

34 BILL: *(Hugging back, but being the first to pull away)* Hey, you
35   OK?

1   **MARY:** I am now that you're here.

2   **BILL:** I just wanted to say hi, see how you were.

3   **MARY:** I'm glad you're here. Stay a while.

4   **BILL:** I can't stay long.

5   **MARY:** My parents aren't here. I don't expect them back for

6   days. They're out of the country. You can stay as long as

7   you like.

8   **BILL:** Oh. Well. So, you doing all right?

9   **MARY:** Yeah. Sort of. You want to sit down with me on the

10   couch?

11   **BILL:** No. Really, I can only stay a minute.

12   **MARY:** Why? No one is here except us. Just us, alone.

13   **BILL:** Yeah. Alone.

14   **MARY:** Don't you want to be alone with me?

15   **BILL:** It's OK. It's fine. Really. Not a problem. So what have

16   you been doing?

17   **MARY:** Doing? You mean since you broke up with me? Since

18   you tore my heart out and threw it on the ground?

19   **BILL:** I guess. Yeah. Uh...

20   **MARY:** Nothing. I've been doing nothing. Eating, watching

21   TV, waiting, hoping for the phone to ring... *(She goes to*

22   *him; he freezes.)*

23   **BILL:** *(Coming out of the scene)* It was so obvious she wasn't

24   over me...

25   **MARY:** *(Coming out of the scene)* It was so obvious he wasn't

26   over me...

27   **BILL:** She looked so pathetic...

28   **MARY:** He looked so angry...

29   **BILL:** So out of it...

30   **MARY:** So lost...

31   **BILL and MARY:** I actually felt sorry about the whole

32   situation...

33   **MARY:** Then he grabbed me. *(She goes back into her version of*

34   *the scene.)* What are you doing?

35   **BILL:** I'm not doing anything I haven't done before.

1 MARY: Listen, Bill, that was before. You have no right to touch
2   me, now or ever.
3 BILL: I told you before, don't tell me what to do.
4 MARY: I'm simply asking you to keep your hands off me.
5 BILL: Since when? Since when do you tell guys to keep their
6   hands off you? You think I didn't hear about you and
7   David? Did you think I'd never hear about it? You
8   can't humiliate me like that and think nothing will
9   happen.
10 MARY: What I do now is none of your business. We broke up.
11   Get over it.
12 BILL: You bitch. You really imagine I can get over us? I never
13   will. You belong to me, now and forever. *(He goes to grab*
14   *her and freezes.)*
15 MARY: *(Coming out of the scene)* I knew I was in big trouble...
16 BILL: *(Coming out of the scene)* Trouble. The girl is trouble.
17 MARY: He was grabbing me, touching me; it made my skin
18   crawl.
19 BILL: She couldn't keep her hands off me. Everytime I moved
20   away from her, she'd follow me, holding me. It was
21   freaking me out. I couldn't get away from her.
22 MARY: *(Back in BILL's version)* The phone never rang. But now
23   you're here and everything will be OK. Won't it?
24 BILL: Listen, Mary. We broke up. You need to get over it.
25   Move on.
26 MARY: Oh, like you have? I heard about you and Caroline. Did
27   you think I wouldn't? Did you think I'd do nothing about
28   it? You can't humiliate me like that and think nothing
29   will happen?
30 BILL: What I do now is none of your business. We broke up.
31   Get over it.
32 MARY: You bastard. You really imagine I can get over us? I
33   never will. You belong to me, now and forever. *(She goes*
34   *to grab him and freezes.)*
35 BILL: It was always that way with her...

1   MARY: He was always like that...
2   BILL: Accusations...
3   MARY: Insinuations...
4   BILL: Constant little remarks...
5   MARY: Little remarks that always sounded like a threat...
6   BILL: A threat. I never knew what she'd do...
7   MARY: He'd do the most bizarre things...
8   BILL: Things that didn't make sense...
9   MARY: Ever since I broke up with him, he's been weird, scary
10   weird...
11   BILL: Ever since I broke up with her, it's scary, how she is. It's
12   hard to explain...
13   MARY: I can't explain it.
14   BILL: *(Back in MARY's version)* I'll never let you go. You know
15   that, don't you? Never.
16   MARY: Bill, I don't know what you expect from me. We were
17   together a long time and our relationship ended. You
18   knew it would. I couldn't allow myself to be treated the
19   way you were treating me.
20   BILL: I treated you how you deserved to be treated. You asked
21   for it.
22   MARY: I *asked* for it? Are you insane? No one asks to be
23   treated like a possession, a thing. I wanted respect and I
24   got abuse.
25   BILL: I respect people who deserve it. You were a lying,
26   cheating, little slut.
27   MARY: I never cheated on you. Ever!
28   BILL: Lying bitch. *(He freezes in mid-slap.)*
29   MARY: *(She comes out of the scene.)* That's how it was — name
30   calling, accusations — then it started into physical
31   abuse...
32   BILL: *(Coming out of the scene)* The abuse took me by
33   surprise. I mean, what's a guy supposed to do? I've never
34   hit a girl in my life, but when you start getting hit, after
35   awhile you have to defend yourself, right?

1   MARY: I never did anything...
2   BILL: Nothing would have made me...
3   MARY: He thought it was fine to take any action...
4   BILL: Actions speak louder than words... *(He goes back into his*
5   *version of the scene.)*
6   MARY: Why are you here?! Did you come to make me feel
7   worse than I already do? Do you get some sort of
8   perverted pleasure in torturing me?
9   BILL: Mary, come on. We were together a long time. I'm
10   concerned. I still have some feelings for you.
11   MARY: Do you? You still have feelings for me?
12   BILL: I would for anyone I cared about.
13   MARY: You still care about me?
14   BILL: Like any friend.
15   MARY: Friend! Friend! Don't do me any favors. I have all the
16   friends I need.
17   BILL: I think I better go.
18   MARY: Fine, get out. *(She shoves him.)* Go! You son of a bitch.
19   Bastard. *(She slaps at him, connecting.)*
20   BILL: *(Fending off MARY's physical attack)* Hey! That's enough.
21   *(He grabs her arms.)* Stop!
22   MARY: *(Grabbing his arms, also)* Stop! *(They both freeze.)*
23   BILL: I told her to stop, but she wouldn't.
24   MARY: He wouldn't. He wouldn't stop. I didn't know what to
25   do...
26   BILL: What would you do? Just stand there?
27   MARY: He's bigger and stronger...
28   BILL: She's stronger than she looks...
29   MARY: He grabbed my hands, I couldn't move...
30   BILL: I had to hold her so she couldn't move...
31   MARY: I was so scared...
32   BILL: I was so scared...
33   MARY: It had never been like this before...
34   BILL: Before it had been just her slapping, but now she was
35   going crazy.

1   MARY: He was crazy. He pinned me down...

2   BILL: She fell down...

3   MARY: I grabbed whatever I could find...

4   BILL: I felt something hit me on the head...

5   MARY: I hit him on the head...

6   BILL: Things went black, just for a second...

7   MARY: I couldn't see what I was doing.

8   BILL: Then there was blood in my eyes...

9   MARY: Then his blood fell on my face...

10 BILL: I had to let her go...

11 MARY: He let me go, just for a second...

12 BILL: She got up...

13 MARY: I got up and tried to get away...

14 BILL: She moved...

15 MARY: He grabbed my leg...

16 BILL: I tried to get up...

17 MARY: I fell back against the table...

18 BILL: I couldn't get up...

19 MARY: It was like a slow-motion movie...

20 BILL: Everything just slowed down. Got blurry...

21 MARY: It's all a blur. I hit the table...

22 BILL: I heard a crack on the table...

23 MARY: My head...

24 BILL: Everything was dark...

25 MARY: I could feel the warm sticky blood...

26 BILL: My blood...

27 MARY: My blood...

28 BILL: There was the loud rushing sound of waves...

29 MARY: Waves of nausea...

30 BILL: Waves of fear...

31 MARY: I looked over at him...

32 BILL: I saw her...

33 MARY: Bleeding...

34 BILL: Bleeding...

35 MARY: How did we get here?

1   **BILL: How did this happen?**
2   **MARY: I looked and then stared...**
3   **BILL: I stared...**
4   **MARY and BILL: And then there was nothing.**
5
6
7
8
9
10
11
12
13
14
15
16
17
18
19
20
21
22
23
24
25
26
27
28
29
30
31
32
33
34
35

Part of the Crowd

(Scene for four men)

1	*(DOMINIC, MATT and JON initiate CHAD into their private*
2	*group.)*
3	**DOMINIC: Stay down, dammit. Be quiet!**
4	**MATT: Hurry up. Jon, come on.**
5	**DOMINIC: We don't have all night.**
6	**MATT: Relax, Dominic.**
7	**DOMINIC: I can't believe we're doing this.**
8	**JON: I'm right behind you. This is too cool.**
9	**DOMINIC: Shut up, dammit. You want people to hear us?**
10	**JON: Whatever. Chad, come on...oh, hell, where's Chad?**
11	**MATT: I thought he was with you.**
12	**JON: He was. He was following me.**
13	**MATT: Well go look for him.**
14	**JON: Screw that. He's on his own.**
15	**DOMINIC: Damn that guy. He could completely ruin this**
16	**whole thing. I told you we shouldn't have brought him.**
17	**MATT: Jon, go get Chad.**
18	**JON: Yeah, OK. I'll get right on that.** *(He sits and gives MATT*
19	*a stare.)*
20	**MATT: Ass.**
21	**JON: Hmmm.**
22	**DOMINIC: I am going to kick the hell out of him. He's been**
23	**holding us up all night.**
24	**MATT: Jon...**
25	**JON: Don't tell me what to do.**
26	**MATT: Fine, I'll get him. God, you are such a...**
27	**CHAD: Hey, where are you guys? Matt? Jon? Dominic?**
28	**DOMINIC: Oh my God, why don't you scream our names at**
29	**the top of your voice. Whose idea was this?**
30	**JON:** *(A nod in MATT's direction)* **His.**
31	**DOMINIC: Chad, shut the hell up and get your butt over here.**
32	**CHAD: I'm coming. It's not easy carrying all this stuff by**
33	**myself, you know. You guys could have helped.**
34	**JON: Yeah, we could have. But since you're the new guy, we**
35	**figured what the hell.**

1   CHAD: Thanks, Jon.
2   JON: Not a problem.
3   MATT: Just set it all down.
4   CHAD: Where?
5   DOMINIC: Anywhere. Just put it down. *(To the others)* I don't
6   know about this. I don't think it's going to work out.
7   MATT: He'll be fine.
8   CHAD: I'll be fine. I will. I want to thank you guys for inviting
9   me to come tonight. This is going to be very cool.
10 JON: Moron.
11 CHAD: What is your problem, Jon?
12 JON: You are my problem. You don't belong.
13 CHAD: Well, Dominic and Matt seem to think I do.
14 MATT: That's right.
15 DOMINIC: What'd you bring?
16 CHAD: Everything you told me to bring.
17 DOMINIC: All of it?
18 CHAD: Uh-huh. I got the tequila from my house, the cigars
19   from a machine, and I found the rope behind the garage.
20 DOMINIC: Good. Very good. You can be counted on.
21 MATT: I told you.
22 JON: I don't trust him.
23 CHAD: I don't know what the deal is with you, but I'm here,
24   I'm staying.
25 JON: Your choice. Remember that. It's your choice.
26 CHAD: I think you just don't want any new blood around.
27   Competition too strong for you, Jon? Can't handle it.
28 JON: Oh, I can handle it. The question is, can you? You have a
29   lot to prove, little man.
30 DOMINIC: Chad, did you bring the knife?
31 CHAD: It's in the bottom of the bag.
32 MATT: OK, break out the tequila, boys.
33 CHAD: I brought glasses, too.
34 JON: Glasses? We don't need no stinking glasses. *(He swigs*
35   *from the bottle.)* Ahhh, what real men are made of.

1   **MATT: Pass that baby here.** *(He, too, drinks from the bottle and*
2   *passes it to DOMINIC.)*
3   **DOMINIC: Yes!** *(He drinks.)*
4   **CHAD: OK, my turn.**
5   **MATT: No, not yet.**
6   **CHAD: What?**
7   **MATT: Not yet.**
8   **DOMINIC: There are rules, my young friend, rules that must**
9   **be obeyed before you can join the big boys. You didn't**
10   **think that you could just join us, did you?**
11   **CHAD: I, uh, I guess I didn't think...**
12   **JON: Didn't think. Why am I not surprised? That's your**
13   **primary barrier in being a part of our little social circle,**
14   **Chad. You don't think. Put your hands behind your back.**
15   **CHAD: Why?**
16   **JON: Are you questioning me?**
17   **CHAD: No...no. I just.**
18   **MATT: Put your hands where he says, Chad.**
19   **CHAD: I...uh...OK.**
20   **DOMINIC: Matt, give me the rope.**
21   **MATT:** *(Looking the rope over)* **Nice rope. Strong rope. Should**
22   **do the trick.**
23   **CHAD: What are you doing?**
24   **JON:** *(Quickly grabbing CHAD)* **A small restraint, that's all. Just**
25   **something to help you keep under control.**
26   **MATT:** *(As he ties CHAD's hands)* **Work with us, Chad boy.**
27   **DOMINIC: You say you want to belong, well this is all a part of**
28   **belonging.**
29   **CHAD: This is just a joke, right?**
30   **DOMINIC:** *(Holding the knife)* **No kidding around here.**
31   **JON: I told you you didn't belong. You wouldn't listen. Well,**
32   **now you're here and there is no turning back. Unless**
33   **you're not man enough to do what it takes.**
34   **CHAD: I'm more a man than you are, Jon.**
35   **JON:** *(Grabbing him)* **Are you? How much of a man are you**

1   now? So you take a drink of tequila. Here, have a cigar.
2   *(He jams one in CHAD's mouth.)* **Feel big now?** *(He slaps*
3   *him across the face.)* **How about now?**
4   DOMINIC: Jon, we can do all that later.
5   MATT: Don't rush into things, man. We've got all night.
6   CHAD: All night for what?
7   JON: For our little ceremony. You could call it an initiation
8   ceremony.
9   DOMINIC: All part of belonging, which is what you say you want.
10   CHAD: Matt, what are you talking about? I thought you were
11   my friend.
12   MATT: Your friend? Chad, you obviously have no idea what
13   the meaning of the word friend is. A friend is someone
14   who will stand up with you, for you and by you. You and
15   I are acquaintances. After tonight, maybe we'll see what
16   kind of a man you are and if you are capable of being a
17   part of our group.
18   JON: I tried to tell you, but you wouldn't listen. You just
19   wanted to be with the big guys. Well, now you're here.
20   DOMINIC: *(Holding out his arm)* See this? This scar? We all
21   have this. You want one? You've got to have it to belong.
22   CHAD: Oh, God.
23   JON: Praying ain't gonna do you any good.
24   MATT: You're lucky, Chad, you know that? We don't invite
25   many people into our circle. But there was something
26   about you. Something I liked.
27   DOMINIC: Hold his arm still.
28   CHAD: Wait. Wait a minute.
29   JON: Losing courage, boy? I knew you would.
30   CHAD: Shut up! Just shut the hell up. I need to think.
31   DOMINIC: There's no thinking involved. You either do it or
32   you don't.
33   JON: You're either one of us or you're not.
34   MATT: You've gone too far to quit. Not now. Not since we
35   brought you here.

1 DOMINIC: This is our secret place. Only a few of us know
2   about it. Just a small group of select guys.
3 JON: You think we could just let you go now? Not a chance.
4   You might tell someone.
5 CHAD: I wouldn't tell anyone.
6 JON: That's what the last guy said.
7 MATT: He told.
8 DOMINIC: What was his name?
9 JON: Derek. His name was Derek Ross.
10 CHAD: I remember him. He came to the school for a few
11   weeks and then, all of a sudden, he was gone...
12 JON: Gone, just like that. I wonder whatever happened to
13   him, don't you, Dominic?
14 DOMINIC: *(Holding the knife under CHAD's chin)* I heard he
15   transferred schools.
16 MATT: That's what the story was. Transferred to Cypress
17   High School. But I have some friends there. They've
18   never seen him.
19 JON: The last person to see him was...Well, wasn't that you,
20   Dominic?
21 DOMINIC: You couldn't prove it in court.
22 CHAD: Oh my God, oh my God.
23 JON: You say something, Chadster?
24 MATT: You don't want to leave, do you?
25 CHAD: Listen. I really think...
26 JON: There he goes, thinking again. *(Shoving him)* You're
27   starting to really annoy me, you know that?
28 MATT: Don't annoy Jon, please. It's not a good thing to
29   annoy Jon.
30 DOMINIC: We're wasting time.
31 CHAD: What are you going to do?
32 DOMINIC: Well, first we have a little fun with you. You drink
33   everything in the bottle, by yourself.
34 CHAD: I thought we were all going to drink.
35 JON: Nah. Why would we want to do that? Drink all that

1   tequila. Nasty drunk, tequila. Makes you sloppy, makes

2   you vomit for hours. I've heard of people actually

3   blacking out. And the hangover is a bad one. Really,

4   really bad.

5   CHAD: I can't drink that whole bottle.

6   MATT: Sure you can. Don't let me down, Chad. I put my

7   reputation on the line getting the guys to accept you. Now

8   you want to make me look like a fool in front of my

9   friends.

10   CHAD: No, I uh...no, but...

11   DOMINIC: But what? Oh, I know, you want to smoke all these

12   cigars first. I should have known. You look like a cigar

13   man. Doesn't he look like a cigar man?

14   CHAD: I don't smoke.

15   JON: Oh, you will tonight.

16   CHAD: I'll get sick.

17   JON: Hell, I wouldn't worry about the cigars. The tequila will

18   probably kill you.

19   MATT: But first you have to get the mark. Dominic is the

20   master of the mark. Two quick slashes on the bicep and

21   it's over.

22   JON: He's really gotten good at it. Especially when he's sober.

23   DOMINIC: *(Taking another drink out of the bottle)* Oops. I

24   forgot I wasn't supposed to drink tonight.

25   CHAD: *(Trying to move away, MATT grabs the rope and pulls.)*

26   Please...

27   MATT: Please what?

28   CHAD: Please don't.

29   DOMINIC: You're not afraid of a little cut, are you? A simple

30   cut. Slash, slash and it's over. If you don't move, it will

31   be fine.

32   CHAD: What if I move?

33   DOMINIC: Let's not talk about it.

34   MATT: Besides, you'll be getting so wasted that you won't

35   care. And with your arms tied up behind you, you'll start

1   to go numb in a little bit anyway.

2   CHAD: I want to go home.

3   JON: I knew it. The baby wants to go home. No one goes home

4   once we start. No one. Got that? No one goes home.

5   CHAD: Please...I won't tell anyone...

6   MATT: Of course you won't. How would you explain this? You

7   came up here on your own.

8   JON: No one held a gun to your head...

9   DOMINIC: Well, maybe a knife to your arm. *(The three laugh*

10   *slyly.)*

11   MATT: You already smell of alcohol. That's the best thing

12   about using tequila. The smell sticks to you.

13   JON: Like the color of blood on a white shirt.

14   DOMINIC: Like the rich, dark smell of a cheap cigar.

15   MATT: Yeah, wait till you start trying to explain this all away.

16   CHAD: I won't have to. I won't have to say a word. I swear.

17   JON: He swears. Oh, I feel secure now. Shut up!

18   CHAD: No, really. You don't understand. I only took a little sip

19   of the tequila. Just a tiny sip. Hardly any at all. We haven't

20   lit up the cigars, so I don't smell of them. And, look,

21   Dominic hasn't cut me yet. So, really, I won't have

22   anything to explain at all. It's all cool.

23   JON: Did you hear that? It's all cool. Well, I don't think it's

24   cool. Dominic, do you think it's cool?

25   DOMINIC: I see nothing cool here.

26   MATT: Cool. Not a word I would choose.

27   CHAD: Guys, really. I won't say anything. Just let me go,

28   please.

29   JON: Are you crying? I think he's crying.

30   MATT: Nah. He wouldn't cry.

31   DOMINIC: Let me take a close look. *(He comes very close with*

32   *the knife.)* Those look like tears in his eyes to me.

33   CHAD: Just let me go, please.

34   DOMINIC: What do you think?

35   MATT: I don't know.

1   JON: Kill him.
2   CHAD: Oh, jeez. I swear guys, I swear to God, I swear on
3   everything in this world that I care about, I won't tell
4   anyone, ever.
5   JON: Kill him.
6   DOMINIC: Jon wants us to kill you. Jon is our friend. You
7   really leave us with no choice.
8   CHAD: No...
9   MATT: Jon, come on. We can let him go, don't you think? I
10   mean, he hasn't seen or heard the real stuff we do.
11   CHAD: There's more?
12   MATT: Do you really want to know?
13   CHAD: No. No! Forget I asked.
14   JON: *(Looking long)* OK.
15   CHAD: *(Almost fainting in relief)* Oh, jeez...
16   JON: But if you ever tell anyone you were here.
17   DOMINIC: If we even think we hear about it...
18   MATT: Guys, there's no need to paint the boy a picture. I
19   think he sees our point. Don't you, Chad? Or should we
20   make it more clear?
21   CHAD: I got it. This never happened. I was never here.
22   MATT: Good boy.
23   JON: I don't want to see you hanging around again, you
24   hear me?
25   CHAD: Yeah...
26   DOMINIC: You stay away from our parties, got that?
27   CHAD: Uh-huh...
28   MATT: Quit hanging out in the parking lot with people you
29   have no business hanging with, understand?
30   CHAD: Yeah, yeah. No parking lot, no parties, no hanging
31   around.
32   JON: Find your own friends, people like you can't handle our
33   crowd, so don't even try.
34   CHAD: Fine, whatever you say.
35   MATT: Get the hell out of here.

1   CHAD: Can you untie me?

2   JON: Kill him...

3   CHAD: No! I'm fine. I can untie this myself later. Don't even

4   worry about it. *(He exits quickly, arms still tied behind him.)*

5   MATT: Run, boy! Run!

6   JON: What a loser.

7   DOMINIC: Well, that was fun.

8   MATT: Jon, got the phone?

9   JON: Right here in my pocket.

10 DOMINIC: You calling now?

11 MATT: Sure. *(He dials.)* Hi, Mrs. Harvey? Yeah, this is Matt.

12   Chad should be on his way home now. No, he's fine.

13   Dominic and Jon and I spoke with the lad. I think he's

14   seen the errors of his ways. We gave him the benefit of

15   our own experiences, and I think he understands where

16   he can go wrong. There won't be any more problems with

17   him hanging out with the wrong crowd. OK. Hey, no

18   problem. Anytime. *(He hangs up.)*

19 JON: This was fun. I wasn't sure it would be, but it turned out

20   to be fun.

21 DOMINIC: What now?

22 MATT: I say we light up these fine cigars and congratulate

23   ourselves on a job well done.

24 JON: It feels good to help out your fellow man, doesn't it?

25 MATT: *(After a moment's reflection, laughing softly)* I thought

26   he was going to pee his pants.

27 DOMNIC: We done good! *(They all laugh.)*

28

29

30

31

32

33

34

35

Perspectives on
FAMILY

Kansas City Stubborn

Finding a Family in the Dark

A Question of Brotherhood

Grandpa

On My Own

Kansas City Stubborn

(Scene for one man and two women)

1   *(ANGELA enters as her mother, MEG, is packing to leave.*

2   *JEFF is off to one side, out of their view.)*

3   **ANGELA: Mom.**

4   **MEG: Yes, honey?**

5   **ANGELA: Why are you doing this?**

6   **MEG: I have to, sweetheart.**

7   **ANGELA: What does that mean, "I have to"? No one wants you**

8   **to go.**

9   **MEG:** *(A sad smile)* **I'm not so sure.**

10   **ANGELA: I don't. Mom, I don't want you to go. I want you here**

11   **with me.**

12   **MEG: I can't stay here. I can't. Not with things the way they**

13   **are. It just wouldn't work.**

14   **ANGELA: But Dad, he loves you. You know he loves you.**

15   **MEG: I love him too, honey.**

16   **ANGELA: Then why leave?**

17   **MEG: Because sometimes just loving someone isn't enough.**

18   **ANGELA: It was enough for twenty years. Why all of a sudden**

19   **isn't it enough now?**

20   **MEG: When you get older, you will understand.**

21   **ANGELA: Mom, I am sixteen years old. I am one year younger**

22   **than you were when you met Dad. Two years from now, I**

23   **could be married with a child, just like you were. Don't**

24   **treat me like a baby, because I'm not.**

25   **MEG: I know that, Angela. It's just very hard to explain. I**

26   **don't really understand it. I just know that it is time for**

27   **me to leave.**

28   **ANGELA: Then why did you even come back home?**

29   **MEG: It's Christmas. You are my family and I wanted to be**

30   **with you.**

31   **ANGELA: That's right. This is your family. You belong here.**

32   **Not with Johnny.**

33   **MEG: I'm not going back to him. At least not tonight.**

34   **ANGELA: You're not?**

35   **MEG: No. I need to be alone for a while. Just a while...**

1   ANGELA: And then you'll come back?

2   MEG: To Johnny.

3   ANGELA: But why him?

4   MEG: Because he needs me. And I guess I need to feel needed.

5   ANGELA: We need you.

6   MEG: No, honey, you don't. You have your life. Your brother
7   has his. You two don't need me anymore.

8   ANGELA: But what about Dad?

9   MEG: He doesn't need me. He used to. Up until a few years
10   ago, when the business wasn't doing well, and he got so
11   sick, then he needed me. Now, he just...

12   ANGELA: Mom, we all want you here.

13   MEG: All? Even your brother?

14   ANGELA: Him most of all. He's hurt, Mom. That's why he's
15   acting this way.

16   MEG: I know. He wants to cause me pain just like he feels I've
17   caused him pain. But there is a difference.

18   ANGELA: There is?

19   MEG: I didn't do it deliberately. I didn't plan for this to
20   happen.

21   JEFF: *(Appearing in the doorway)* Is that so? Well, either way,
22   suffering is suffering, isn't it, Mom?

23   MEG: *(Standing tall, looking at him levelly)* Yes, Jeff, it is.
24   Suffering is suffering. And each of us will deal with it in
25   our own way.

26   JEFF: No matter who it continues to hurt.

27   MEG: *(Maintains eye contact for a moment longer, then turns*
28   *back to her packing.)* I'll be gone in a few minutes.

29   ANGELA: Don't go, Mom. Please.

30   JEFF: Let her, sis. She isn't wanted here...

31   ANGELA: I want her here...

32   JEFF: I said let her go. Back to her boyfriend. Right, Mom?
33   Isn't Johnny at home waiting for you? Hey, it was real
34   great of him to let you come on over here for Christmas
35   dinner with the old family. Swell guy. But now you go on

1   back to him. Just leave us...again.

2   MEG: You haven't any idea, do you, of what I'm going
3   through?

4   JEFF: Gee, no, Mom. I guess when Dad broke down and cried
5   in my arms the night you left, I just sort of lost track of
6   how you and your new boyfriend must have felt. Guess
7   I'm just pretty damn selfish, huh? Like mother, like son,
8   or so they say.

9   MEG: You have no right to talk to me this way. To treat me
10   with so little respect.

11   JEFF: Why? Because you're my mother? Well, you should have
12   thought of that before you started screwing around.
13   *(MEG walks slowly and deliberately to him, looks him in*
14   *the eye and then slaps him across the face. After a moment*
15   *of tense silence)* It seems appropriate that the last time
16   you will ever touch me, you slap me across the face. *(He*
17   *smiles without humor.)* Yeah, pretty fitting. *(To ANGELA)*
18   I'll be in my room. Let me know when she leaves. *(He*
19   *starts to leave.)*

20   MEG: Jeff, I'm sorry. I didn't...

21   JEFF: *(At the door, turns on her viciously.)* What, you didn't
22   mean to? You don't mean a lot of things, do you? You
23   don't mean to hurt us, and then you leave. You don't
24   mean to cause any more pain, but then you come over
25   here for Christmas dinner and leave again. You said you
26   loved us, but obviously you didn't mean that either.

27   ANGELA: Jeff, that's enough. You can't talk to Mom this way.

28   JEFF: I'll talk to her any way I please. Why shouldn't I?

29   ANGELA: Because I won't allow it.

30   JEFF: Allow it? What does that mean? Allow it? Don't tell me
31   what I will and will not say, either of you.

32   MEG: Angela, let him say what he has to say. He needs to get
33   this out.

34   JEFF: Oh, isn't that just like you. Good old Mom. Good old,
35   come-to-me-whenever-you-need-me-Mom. I-will-always-

1   be-there-for-you Mom. Well, Mom, lately I've been
2   looking, and guess what? You're not there. You're with
3   your boyfriend.
4 MEG: And when was the last time you ever wanted me when
5   I wasn't there for you? Never. That's when.
6 JEFF: You're not here now, are you? Oh, you're here for the
7   night, but as soon as Dad gets back with the cab, you'll
8   be gone.
9 MEG: You won't even try to understand, will you?
10 JEFF: There is nothing to understand, Mom.
11 MEG: Just listen to me for a minute. Hear me out. I will try to
12   explain this to you.
13 JEFF: You can't explain this. Nothing you can say will ever
14   explain it to me. *(There is a silence, finally broken by*
15   *ANGELA, who speaks quietly.)*
16 ANGELA: I want to understand why you left. I need to know.
17   What was so terrible here that you couldn't stay?
18 MEG: Nothing was terrible.
19 ANGELA: But then, why?
20 MEG: Nothing was terrible, and yet nothing was great.
21   Everything just was...
22 ANGELA: Was what?
23 MEG: Just was. No highs, no lows, just going along.
24 JEFF: You mean life? Normal everyday life just wasn't for
25   you, huh?
26 MEG: I've never been able to live that way. Your father knew
27   that from the first.
28 ANGELA: Knew what?
29 MEG: That I needed more in my life than a daily routine. I
30   have never done what others do. And your father knew it.
31   That's what he loved about me.
32 ANGELA: He still loves you.
33 MEG: He loves what he thinks he sees. I'm not the woman I've
34   been pretending to be for the last few years. I'm still that
35   girl he married twenty years ago. I've learned that.

1   JEFF: Twenty years is a long time.
2   MEG: A long time to you. Not to me. It doesn't seem so very
3   long ago that I was young...but to you, it must. We got
4   married when I was still seventeen. I may have been
5   young, but I was so strong. Stubborn. Kansas City
6   stubborn. I took one look at your father and said, I'm
7   gonna marry that man. *(She laughs softly, smiling at the*
8   *memory.)* He didn't stand a chance. Yes, we were young,
9   and everyone warned us, but we were going to be
10   different. We were going to "make it!" And then, I was
11   twenty, had a son, pregnant with you, Angela, and money
12   was tight. But you know, I didn't care. I knew we would
13   be all right, because I was going to see to it.
14   JEFF: *(Without admiration)* You always get what you want,
15   don't you?
16   MEG: No, Jeff, I don't. But God knows I try.
17   ANGELA: Mom, I know it was hard. And I know how much
18   you and Dad worked to make a living, to build a life for this
19   family. That's why I don't see how you could just leave.
20   MEG: I think that a lot of it had to do with just that. The fact
21   that your father and I spent so much time making a
22   living for you two and "a family," that when we turned
23   around and finally took a look at each other, and
24   ourselves, I didn't like what I saw anymore.
25   JEFF: What happened to the determined "I'm gonna marry
26   that man"?
27   MEG: I had put her on ice for a while. That woman had to be
28   quiet and build a life for her husband and children. One
29   day, I was walking down Spring Street and saw a woman
30   in the window. I thought, "Put a little makeup on her,
31   fix her hair and get her a nicer dress, she wouldn't be
32   bad looking."
33   ANGELA: You have always done that. Looked at other women
34   and dressed them up in your mind.
35   MEG: But this time, I got scared. The woman was me. I was

1   looking at a reflection of myself. I was only thirty-seven,
2   but the woman in the window looked fifty.
3 JEFF: So get a new hair style, get a new dress, get a new
4   boyfriend. I see how it works.
5 ANGELA: Jeff, could you shut up for a while, just once and let
6   Mom talk?
7 JEFF: That's all I hear is talk. I still don't understand.
8 MEG: I don't think you will. I don't. I just know that all of a
9   sudden, one day, the girl was gone and in her place was a
10   woman. An unhappy woman. And I don't even know how
11   she got here.
12 ANGELA: But why? Is Dad so different now, too?
13 MEG: He changed. I changed. Everything is different.
14 ANGELA: That's not true. Dad loves you.
15 MEG: I know that. But we didn't have anything to say to each
16   other. *(To JEFF)* And then you and he would go out
17   bowling or to a game every night. I guess he was trying to
18   make up for the early years of working so much and not
19   spending enough time with you. And there I was. Alone.
20 ANGELA: I was there.
21 MEG: I know, sweetheart, but it's not the same. I would sit in
22   the house day after day. I had just turned thirty-seven,
23   and I was old. My own children grown up, my husband
24   and I rarely spoke. And I thought, when did this new
25   party start and why didn't anyone tell me about it? Was I
26   the only one in the world who hadn't been invited?
27 ANGELA: Why didn't you say something?
28 MEG: Because I was not raised to say anything. My mother
29   always told me, "Meg, look your troubles in the eye, and
30   then if they don't get out of your way, walk right through
31   them." So, that's what I did. But I don't think she would
32   be very proud to know about the way I walked.
33 JEFF: You mean you left Dad because he was spending time
34   with me?
35 MEG: It's not that simple.

1   JEFF: It seems so to me. I could see it if he were cheating on
2   you. Oh, but wait...you did that.
3   ANGELA: Jeff!
4   MEG: I didn't mean for it to happen, Jeff.
5   JEFF: But it did, didn't it? Yeah, I can see how you must have
6   felt. Dad treating you so rotten because he was with his
7   son, being a good father. I can understand how you
8   would feel justified in sleeping with another man.
9   MEG: That's enough!
10   JEFF: Not nearly.
11   MEG: I said that's enough. I will not let you speak to me like
12   this. What I did was wrong, fine. I won't deny it. But it
13   wasn't cheap. I love Johnny. We are going to be married.
14   ANGELA: What?!
15   JEFF: Married?! You can't be serious.
16   ANGELA: How can you love Johnny? You say you still love
17   Dad.
18   MEG: I do love him. But it could never be what it was. He will
19   never look at me again without thinking about Johnny.
20   ANGELA: Mom, stay. Please. You saw the way Dad was looking
21   at you tonight. You know he would take you back.
22   MEG: I can't. I couldn't settle for less than what we had.
23   ANGELA: *(Desperately)* He wants you to come back. I want you
24   to come back.
25   MEG: I can't. There's too much that's happened. I betrayed
26   him in the worst possible way and now the thought of
27   him looking at me and seeing the mistrust in his
28   eyes...no. I can't.
29   ANGELA: But...
30   JEFF: Wait a minute. Wait just one minute. *(To ANGELA)* You
31   would seriously want her back in this house? After she
32   has left her husband, her kids, been living with a man
33   who is not her husband?
34   ANGELA: Yes! She's my mother. She belongs here.
35   JEFF: No, she does not. Not anymore. She gave up that part of

1   her life the day she walked out. Sometimes there is no
2   turning back once a decision has been made.
3   ANGELA: But the decision hasn't been made.
4   JEFF: *(Looking at his mother)* Yes, Angela, it has. *(To MEG)* I
5   used to think there was no one on this earth whom I
6   could trust more than you. I thought you were
7   everything a woman should be. You were the woman I
8   measured against every other female in the world, and
9   all of them came up short next to you. All of them. The
10   same thing with you and Dad. I told everyone that I
11   wanted to get married to someone like you and have the
12   same kind of life. *(His voice begins to rise.)* And it was all
13   a lie, wasn't it? Your whole life together has been nothing
14   but one lie after the other. Everything I ever believed in
15   was just a lie.
16   MEG: *(Her voice rising to meet his)* No! It wasn't! It wasn't! *(In*
17   *the silence, crying softly)* It wasn't, Jeff.
18   ANGELA: *(Going to MEG)* It's OK, Mom. It's OK.
19   JEFF: No. It's not OK. And it never will be again.
20   MEG: All right. Fine. But that is your decision, not mine...
21   JEFF: Oh, but it was, Mom. The day you walked out of this
22   house, the decision was made.
23   MEG: Listen...
24   JEFF: *(Begins walking out of the room.)* You have nothing to
25   say that I want to hear...
26   MEG: *Sit down! (He looks at her, and slowly walks back into the*
27   *room to sit.)* You're right about one thing: I made a
28   decision when I walked out, but it had nothing to do with
29   you kids. It doesn't even have anything to do with your
30   father. It's me. All me. I was the one who was unhappy. I
31   was the one who felt unloved and alone. And I was
32   scared. I'm only thirty-seven. It really isn't that old, when
33   you think about it. But I looked at you two, all grown up.
34   I looked at this house, and I looked at my life and I
35   thought I'm done. No one needs me to do anything

1   anymore. And suddenly, I needed to dance. I had to feel
2   young again. When Vera invited me to join her at the club
3   dances, I told your father about it. I wanted to go, but he
4   said no. He hates to dance. Funny, he didn't used to. He
5   told me to go. So I did. And I met Johnny. He loved to
6   dance, and laugh, and sing. He made me feel young
7   again. And he needs me.
8 ANGELA: Dad needs you, too.
9 MEG: No. He just loves me. But he doesn't depend on me like
10   Johnny will. And for some reason, I like being depended
11   on.
12 JEFF: I depended on you. Did me a helluva lot of good.
13 MEG: Say what you want. I won't stop you.
14 JEFF: I don't have anymore to say, except this: If you leave us
15   tonight, I don't want to see you again. Ever. And I mean it.
16 MEG: *(Going to him)* Honey, I don't...
17 JEFF: *(Backing away)* That's all I have to say. *(As he is leaving,*
18   *with his back to her, quietly)* I mean this, Mom. If you
19   leave, I will never see you again. *(He exits.)*
20 MEG: *(Emotionally spent, sadly sarcastic)* Well, that went well,
21   don't you think?
22 ANGELA: He didn't mean...
23 MEG: Yes, he did. And I guess I deserved it. He will never
24   understand. No one will. I don't. *(She continues her packing.)*
25 ANGELA: So what are you going to do?
26 MEG: I'm going away for a while.
27 ANGELA: But not back to Johnny's tonight?
28 MEG: Not tonight, no.
29 ANGELA: Talk to Dad. Try to work things out.
30 MEG: I did.
31 ANGELA: You did? When?
32 MEG: While you and Jeff were in the kitchen.
33 ANGELA: He loves you, right? And he wants you to come back,
34   doesn't he?
35 MEG: Yes.

1 ANGELA: You are, aren't you? After you go away for a while?
2   You'll come back, won't you?
3 MEG: No, honey, I can't. A few years ago I could never have
4   thought that I would leave your father. But so many little
5   things happen. Things so small that you don't notice
6   them even taking place. And then one day it's too late.
7   And you don't know when or why it happened. It just did.
8 ANGELA: So you fix it.
9 MEG: It's not that simple. If it were, I would still be here. But
10   it's not.
11 ANGELA: I don't know why it's not. What about love? Isn't
12   love enough?
13 MEG: Let me try to explain it to you. For the longest time, the
14   thing I loved best about your father was the way he
15   looked at me. His eyes were so clear, and he looked
16   straight at me, hiding nothing. And then he stopped
17   looking at me altogether. It wasn't his fault. We stopped
18   looking at each other. But tonight, I thought, try. Just try
19   to see if anything was still there.
20 ANGELA: Wasn't it there? He put his arm around you in front
21   of the tree. You kissed him. There had to be something.
22 MEG: Yes, there was. And then I looked into his eyes, and he
23   looked away. Just for a second, but he looked away. When
24   he looked back at me, his eyes weren't clear. They were a
25   little sad, a little clouded. And I knew then, I couldn't live
26   with that.
27 ANGELA: Live with what?
28 MEG: The distrust, the sadness. Oh, we would try to make it
29   be all right. But it would never be the pure love we used
30   to have. And I couldn't have less than that with your
31   father. It would be too painful.
32 ANGELA: And you have it with Johnny now?
33 MEG: No. But it's OK. I won't miss it with him because it was
34   never there. But with your father...no. I couldn't take it.
35   *(Having completed her packing, she picks up the bag.)* I

1   have to go now, honey.

2   ANGELA: Do you?

3   MEG: Yes...I really do.

4   ANGELA: Where are you going?

5   MEG: Back home to Kansas City for a few weeks.

6   ANGELA: Why there?

7   MEG: I need to find someone, see if she's OK.

8   ANGELA: Who?

9   MEG: Me. Somewhere along the road, I got very lost.

10   ANGELA: Will you call when you get back?

11   MEG: If you want me to.

12   ANGELA: No matter what, you are still my mother.

13   MEG: Thank you, sweetheart.

14   ANGELA: I'll see what I can do about Jeff.

15   MEG: No. He needs to work through this thing in his own way.

16   He's a lot like me. Look those troubles in the eye and then

17   walk through them. *(Touching ANGELA's face)* You have

18   always been more like your father. Sweet, innocent, too

19   forgiving for your own good.

20   ANGELA: I'll be OK, Mom. Will you?

21   MEG: I don't know. I really don't know. But I'm gonna give it

22   my best shot. *(She begins to leave.)* Take care of both of

23   them, OK?

24   ANGELA: I will. I love you, Mom.

25   MEG: I love you, too, honey. *(And she is gone. ANGELA stands*

26   *in the room alone, and then exits through the door, going*

27   *off in the opposite direction her mother went.)*

28

29

30

31

32

33

34

35

Finding a Family in the Dark

(Scene for two men and two women)

1   (Sisters KIRSTEN and SHAY at their home trying to decide
2   on the plans for the evening with their friends JEFF and
3   JAMES.)
4   KIRSTEN: What do you guys want to do tonight?
5   SHAY: I don't know. Jeff, what do you think?
6   JEFF: *(Preoccupied)* I don't care.
7   KIRSTEN: *(Exchanging a look with JAMES and SHAY)* How
8   about a movie?
9   JAMES: That sounds good.
10   JEFF: Whatever.
11   KIRSTEN: They're showing a restored version of *Casablanca*
12   at the Capri Theatre.
13   SHAY: That's my favorite old movie. Jeff, what do you say?
14   JEFF: Great, an old movie about a woman who cheats on her
15   husband and he takes her back. Yeah, let's all troop off to
16   that one.
17   KIRSTEN: Your vote is no, I take it.
18   JEFF: You take it right.
19   JAMES: We could go dancing.
20   JEFF: I don't feel like it.
21   JAMES: How about ice skating? Jeff, you love to ice skate.
22   SHAY: Oh, Jeff, we could hold hands and just float along to
23   the music.
24   JEFF: Same as dancing. No thanks.
25   SHAY: You OK, honey?
26   JEFF: I'm fine, OK? I just have some things to think about.
27   KIRSTEN: Tonight? You have to think about your *things* tonight?
28   JAMES: Jeff, buddy, come on. There must be something you'd
29   like to do that would be fun.
30   JEFF: I don't know, James. I guess I'm just not in a fun mood.
31   You guys decide.
32   KIRSTEN: Well, we could sit here and listen to you whine all
33   night. We're all getting accustomed to spending our
34   evenings that way.
35   SHAY: Kirsten, shut up.

1   KIRSTEN: It's the truth and you know it.

2   SHAY: Jeff's been upset lately. You know that.

3   JAMES: Come on, girls, let's not fight.

4   KIRSTEN: We're not fighting. We're sisters discussing a topic.

5   And the topic of discussion is Jeff and his moods.

6   JEFF: Am I or am I not still in the room? Why am I being

7   referred to in the third person?

8   KIRSTEN: Well, we might as well. Your body is here, but lately

9   your mind is miles away.

10   JEFF: Maybe I should join it.

11   KIRSTEN: Maybe you should.

12   SHAY: Now that's enough from both of you.

13   KIRSTEN: Listen, little sister, don't start telling me what

14   to do.

15   SHAY: I'm not. I'm simply trying to avoid a confrontation.

16   KIRSTEN: Do what you do best.

17   SHAY: And what does that mean?

18   KIRSTEN: Nothing. Sorry. Really, I am. OK, Jeff?

19   JEFF: I'm just gonna go. It's pretty obvious that I'm bringing

20   everyone down.

21   JAMES: You don't have to go. Just stay for a while and you'll

22   feel better. Trust me.

23   JEFF: I don't trust anyone anymore.

24   KIRSTEN: *(Under her breath)* Here we go.

25   JEFF: I heard that.

26   SHAY: Forget about it, both of you. James, get the paper and

27   see what's playing at the Cinedome.

28   JEFF: What did you mean "Here we go"?

29   KIRSTEN: It's the same old same old. Your parents are

30   splitting up. Well, I'm sorry. James, did Shay and I

31   become this annoyingly despondent when our parents

32   got divorced?

33   SHAY: Let's not go there, OK?

34   KIRSTEN: I'm asking James for a simple comparison. Well?

35   JAMES: Not when I knew you. But I wasn't there for the first

1   divorce. I came into the picture for the second one.

2   KIRSTEN: OK, but when my mom divorced your dad, we

3   didn't go down the emotional toilet, did we?

4   JAMES: Nah. That was my dad's third divorce. No big deal

5   by then.

6   SHAY: I think Mom is having problems with Nick. They fight

7   all the time. I heard her call her attorney yesterday

8   morning.

9   KIRSTEN: There! You see! She's probably getting divorced

10   again. I'm fine with it, so is Shay. How about you, James?

11   JAMES: I'm not officially in the family anymore, but speaking

12   as a former stepbrother and now as a friend, I never

13   really liked Nick.

14   KIRSTEN: Shay, you?

15   SHAY: I just don't pay attention anymore.

16   KIRSTEN: You see, Jeff? You get used to it.

17   JEFF: Do you people hear yourselves? Two, three, four

18   divorces. It doesn't even phase you. It's been going on

19   with your parents in some form or another for years,

20   since you were kids. But I am seventeen and, sorry, but

21   I'm a virgin in this field. After twenty years my mom and

22   dad are divorcing. So sorry if my entire world and

23   everything I believed in is crashing down around me and

24   I am a bit blue about it. How selfish of me.

25   SHAY: Jeff, sweetheart, it's OK.

26   JEFF: It's not OK. Nothing will be OK ever again.

27   KIRSTEN: Get over yourself.

28   JAMES: Oh boy.

29   KIRSTEN: I'm serious. So your parents are divorcing. What

30   does that have to do with you?

31   JAMES: Kirsten, that's enough.

32   SHAY: Just shut up, all right? You've said plenty.

33   JEFF: Shay, I'll be outside. I can't be in here anymore with

34   your sister. Her empathy for my problems is just

35   overwhelming.

1   SHAY: *(She goes to him to hug him.)* **Are you crying?**

2   JEFF: *(Looking pointedly at KIRSTEN)* **Is it allowed?** *(He exits.)*

3   SHAY: **Well, I hope you're happy.**

4   JAMES: **Jeez, Kirsten. Do you think you could have been any**

5   **more sensitive?**

6   KIRSTEN: **Get past it, that's what I say. Good grief, he acts like**

7   **he's the only person on earth whose parents have split**

8   **up. It happens to everyone.**

9   JAMES: **He has a point, you know. Our parents all started**

10   **their adventures in divorce when we were really young.**

11   **We're used to it.**

12   SHAY: **Are we? Kirsten, are we?**

13   KIRSTEN: **What does that mean?**

14   SHAY: **I will never forget when Mom and Dad first separated.**

15   **How old were we then?**

16   KIRSTEN: **You were six and I was seven.**

17   SHAY: **I remember crawling into your bed the night Mom**

18   **told us that Dad was gone. Both of us just cried and cried**

19   **because our daddy was not going to live with us**

20   **anymore.**

21   JAMES: **When my dad married your mom I was so happy. I**

22   **mean, my mom is kind of a nut case. Damn, she couldn't**

23   **sign those papers fast enough to give up any kind of**

24   **custody on me. When I became a part of this family I felt**

25   **secure for the first time. Two built-in sisters, a mom who**

26   **actually hugged me like she wasn't worried I'd mess her**

27   **hair and makeup. But then the first time my dad left your**

28   **mom and he took me with him, God, that was hell. Just**

29   **plain hell. I could never understand what happened**

30   **between them.**

31   KIRSTEN: **Face it, it's easier to give up than to try. Sometimes**

32   **the effort just isn't worth the result.**

33   SHAY: **The result is family.**

34   KIRSTEN: **Yeah, but what kind of family?**

35   SHAY: **Well, at least your dad stayed in the neighborhood so**

1   you could still be close to us.
2   JAMES: And I still have your mom around me. Maybe not in the
3   same house, but she's there. At least I can count on her.
4   KIRSTEN: I'm glad *you* can.
5   SHAY: We all can, Kirsten.
6   KIRSTEN: Yeah, right, terrific.
7   SHAY: We can!
8   KIRSTEN: The only thing I can count on is that every three
9   years or so there will be a new man to call uncle
10   whatever, then a new hideous bridesmaid dress that I
11   can never wear again.
12   SHAY: Talk about getting over yourself.
13   KIRSTEN: I'm serious. Mom's a flake when it comes to men.
14   Our dad's no better in his marital choices. Marriage is a
15   joke. One huge joke that's played on the kids.
16   JAMES: Oh, no, Kirsten hasn't been affected by divorce at all.
17   She's a mental rock.
18   KIRSTEN: Screw you, James.
19   SHAY: I thought you were all fine with everything.
20   KIRSTEN: Well, I'm not, OK? I'm not. Look at what we've
21   grown up seeing. Marriage, divorce, divorce, marriage.
22   Hell, it would have been easier if they'd died.
23   SHAY: I can't believe you said that!
24   KIRSTEN: It's true! At least that's something stable. Death is
25   final, there are no questions, no guessing. Gone is gone
26   with death. With divorce, gone can come back in some
27   different scary form.
28   JAMES: You'd rather your parents were dead?
29   KIRSTEN: Yeah.
30   JAMES: Whoa. That's pretty heavy.
31   SHAY: If you feel this way, why didn't you ever say anything?
32   I'm your sister, for God's sake. I've been through all this
33   with you.
34   KIRSTEN: You know my motto: Get past it.
35   JAMES: Sounds like it's more: Suppress it.

1   KIRSTEN: Either way. How I feel is my business. I shouldn't
2   have said what I did to you guys. It's my problem.
3   SHAY: No, it's a family problem.
4   KIRSTEN: You show me a family and I will share my problem.
5   All I see is one little sister and a stepbrother.
6   JEFF: *(Entering)* How about a friend?
7   KIRSTEN: Now we can add eavesdropping to your other
8   qualities of self-pity and whining.
9   JEFF: Say what you want, Kirsten, but you feel exactly as I feel.
10 KIRSTEN: Oh, and how is that?
11 JEFF: Betrayed.
12 SHAY: Yeah, betrayed. I don't understand why people get
13   divorced.
14 JAMES: My dad says he grew apart from his wives.
15 JEFF: That's what my mom said.
16 SHAY: I don't understand. If they loved each other enough to
17   get married and have kids, how did they stop loving
18   each other?
19 KIRSTEN: I don't know. I do know, though, that I will never get
20   married and put my kids through something like this.
21 JEFF: Me, either.
22 SHAY: Not me. I'll get married, but I will never get divorced,
23   ever. Not if I have kids.
24 JAMES: Are you saying you'd stay in a bad marriage for "the
25   sake of the children"?
26 SHAY: No. What I would do is make sure my marriage stayed
27   good.
28 JAMES: But what if you stop loving that person?
29 SHAY: I guess I will just have to remember why I loved him to
30   begin with and work with that. Plus, I will make
31   absolutely sure that the guy I marry feels the same way.
32 KIRSTEN: Shay, when you pop back from your trip over the
33   rainbow through Never Never Land, please let us know.
34   I'm sure we'd all love to see the slides of Fantasy World.
35 JEFF: Shay, don't delude yourself. I thought my parents had

1   the perfect marriage, and now look. Separated, my mom
2   is living with some guy, my dad is dating. Nothing lasts.
3   Nothing.
4 JAMES: Some marriages do.
5 KIRSTEN: Yeah, one in a million.
6 SHAY: Grandma and Grandpa. Nana and Pawpaw. James,
7   your grandparents are still together, aren't they? Why?
8 KIRSTEN: From a different time, when people committed to
9   something, they stayed committed.
10 SHAY: Why can't we? So our parents screwed up an entire
11   generation. We don't have to.
12 JAMES: The people of the sixties were a weird group.
13 KIRSTEN: Well, for heaven's sake, look at their clothes. How
14   can you expect to be taken seriously dressed in beads,
15   bell-bottom pants, long hair parted down the middle and
16   ruffled collars? And that was the men!
17 JEFF: Shay has a point, though. So our parents were part of
18   that me-me-me-I-I-I generation.
19 JAMES: You know, I remember my mom saying to me, right
20   after she told me that she wasn't going to take joint
21   custody, that she had to "find herself." Find herself. I
22   thought "what does that mean?" So, while she went off to
23   look for herself, she lost me along the way. She lost me.
24 KIRSTEN: But we found you. I guess we make families where
25   we can.
26 JEFF: I guess. God, this sucks, though. There is this huge dark
27   empty hole where my family used to be. It feels like it will
28   never be full again.
29 SHAY: Jeff, I'm here for you.
30 JEFF: But for how long? How long will our relationship last?
31 SHAY: I don't know. I'm only sixteen and too young to
32   promise you anything more than today and maybe
33   tomorrow. But I do promise this: As long as we are honest
34   with each other, we will always be friends. Maybe we
35   won't be in love, but we can always love each other.

1 JAMES: One thing my dad did say to me, the only thing that
2   ever made sense, was: "Real family are people you can
3   count on." Maybe here, in this room, is all the family I
4   need for now.
5 KIRSTEN: Yeah, maybe.
6 SHAY: As long as we are committed to being there for each
7   other, maybe this is as good as it gets.
8 KIRSTEN: Jeff, can you fill a little of that dark empty hole
9   with us?
10 JEFF: Yeah. I think I can.
11 JAMES: Let's make a vow right here that we will always be
12   there for each other.
13 KIRSTEN: Pretty deep for a guy, James, don'tcha think?
14 SHAY: Very supportive, Kirsten.
15 KIRSTEN: I'm kidding. Defense mechanism.
16 JEFF: OK, let's do this on a try-out.
17 SHAY: What?
18 JEFF: What I mean is, we vow to be committed to one another
19   for one year. Let's see if we can make it one year.
20 JAMES: You mean like a contract with options.
21 JEFF: Yeah.
22 SHAY: Wait a minute. Either we commit to being friends or
23   we don't. This is what we just got through ragging on our
24   parents about. Commitment is commitment, or it's just
25   one more temporary arrangement. I, for one, am tired of
26   temporary arrangements. I just told you, Jeff, that as long
27   as we are honest with each other, we'll be friends. That's
28   a commitment. If you can't do it, then say so. If you can,
29   then it's going to be something that you'll have to work
30   at. I'm willing.
31 JAMES: Me, too, I guess.
32 SHAY: It can't be a guess. It's a yes or no thing.
33 JAMES: *(After a moment)* OK, I'm in.
34 JEFF: Me, too.
35

1   **SHAY:** Kirsten?

2   **KIRSTEN:** I don't know if I can.

3   **SHAY:** Try. Just make up your mind to do it.

4   **KIRSTEN:** *(She looks at all of them, one by one.)* **Yeah, OK.**

5   **SHAY:** Together we make our own family, starting right here.

6   Commitment.

7   **JEFF:** Commitment.

8   **JAMES:** Commitment.

9   **KIRSTEN:** *(Deep breath, then)* **Commitment.**

10

11

12

13

14

15

16

17

18

19

20

21

22

23

24

25

26

27

28

29

30

31

32

33

34

35

A Question of Brotherhood

(Scene for three men)

1   *(TONY and LUKE confront their younger brother STEVEN*

2   *about his unconforming attitudes about life.)*

3   **STEVEN:** *(Plays the guitar, singing softly, almost to himself.*

4   *After a moment, he notices TONY and LUKE watching*

5   *him.)* **I didn't see you.**

6   **TONY:** I guess not.

7   **STEVEN:** *(Plays for another moment or two, then)* **What?**

8   **TONY:** Nothing.

9   **LUKE:** You missed a raging party.

10   **STEVEN:** *(Not interested)* **Yeah?**

11   **TONY:** Yeah. It was great. You would have had a great time.

12   Brianne was there.

13   **STEVEN:** So?

14   **TONY:** She asked if you were going to be there. I told her yes.

15   We looked pretty stupid when you didn't show up.

16   **LUKE:** She was waiting for you. It could have been your lucky

17   night. Brianne is one hot chick.

18   **STEVEN:** Great. Brianne doesn't give me the time of day at

19   school and now she's waiting for me to show up at a

20   party. I don't think so. I'm not into these casual macs

21   anyway.

22   **LUKE:** When's the last time you got together with a girl?

23   **STEVEN:** Why is it your business?

24   **LUKE:** I'm just asking.

25   **STEVEN:** And I'm not answering.

26   **LUKE:** Because you've got nothing to say. You've never gotten

27   together with anyone, have you?

28   **STEVEN:** Why are we talking about this?

29   **TONY:** He has. He's with Melissa all the time.

30   **STEVEN:** She's just a friend.

31   **TONY:** Well, what about Lisa?

32   **STEVEN:** What about her?

33   **TONY:** You've macked with her.

34   **STEVEN:** No.

35   **LUKE:** Everyone else has, why not you?

1   STEVEN: Because she's a friend. And I don't just get together
2   for the sake of getting together with a girl. That's not my
3   style. And I wouldn't talk about it anyway.
4   LUKE: Sissy boy. You sit in this room or in the quad at school
5   playing that damn guitar and doing nothing about it.
6   What an idiot.
7   TONY: Really. Steven, you are passing up a golden opportunity.
8   STEVEN: What the hell are you talking about?
9   LUKE: Chicks. They love guys who can sing and play the
10   guitar.
11   TONY: It's like the ultimate aphrodisiac.
12   STEVEN: Get real.
13   TONY: Don't you watch the girls when you play? They all
14   gather around and sigh. You could do any of them. Even
15   Brianne thinks you're cool when you sing.
16   LUKE: But she comes back to her senses the minute you stop.
17   She sees it's just Steven again, and she's back with a
18   football player where she belongs. Not with some pansy
19   "artiste."
20   STEVEN: Get out of my room. Conversation's over.
21   LUKE: We'll leave when we're ready.
22   STEVEN: Do what you want. I'm ignoring you. *(He plays for a*
23   *while, then)* Why are you guys staring at me?
24   TONY: I'm not staring. I'm watching.
25   LUKE: Just watching.
26   STEVEN: Watching what?
27   TONY: Watching our brother turn into a sissy boy right in
28   front of our eyes.
29   STEVEN: Oh, jeez, here we go.
30   LUKE: Where the hell were you tonight?
31   TONY: We waited for you in the parking lot at school and you
32   never showed.
33   LUKE: What's up with that?
34   STEVEN: Nothing is up with that. I didn't feel like going to
35   some lame jock-infested drunken party.

1   TONY: Then where were you?

2   STEVEN: Here.

3   LUKE: Here. All night? You just sat here?

4   STEVEN: That's right. Playing my guitar.

5   TONY: Why didn't you show up at Marshall's party?

6   STEVEN: Because I didn't feel like it.

7   TONY: You felt like staying home instead? Yeah, Steven, that
8   makes tons of sense.

9   LUKE: Hey, he's turning into more of a freak every day.

10   STEVEN: Leave me alone, OK?

11   TONY: No, I won't leave you alone. What the hell is your
12   problem? I don't understand you at all.

13   LUKE: I gave up trying to understand him.

14   STEVEN: You never even tried.

15   TONY: Try? Hell, I've been trying all my life. So has Dad and
16   Luke. You're just weird.

17   STEVEN: Why? Because I'm not a clone of my brothers and
18   father? Because I'd rather read a book than run a race?
19   Because I'd rather compose music than play football?

20   LUKE: Because you'd rather sit alone with a guitar in your
21   hands than sit in the dark with a woman in your arms.
22   Now that's weird.

23   STEVEN: Not every guy wants to mac down with any woman
24   who happens to be near, you know. Not every guy in the
25   world is like you...

26   LUKE: True, "Mary Jane," there are those guys who don't
27   really care for women.

28   TONY: He likes women. Steven, you like women, right?

29   LUKE: He'd rather be around his weirdo friends. All the
30   fruits and nuts.

31   STEVEN: What is your problem? Why is it that because I don't
32   like sports, that I like art, music and theatre, I actually
33   *enjoy* reading, why does that automatically give you the
34   right to decide who and what I am?

35   TONY: No one is deciding what you are.

1   LUKE: I am. He's a woman.

2   STEVEN: Shut up, Luke.

3   LUKE: You gonna make me? Come on, be a man. For once in

4   your life, be a man. *(He pushes STEVEN.)*

5   STEVEN: Stop it.

6   LUKE: *(Mocking STEVEN)* Stop it. Stop it. *(Regular voice)* Is the

7   fruit fly scared? Is the big bad jock brother scaring the

8   little art boy?

9   STEVEN: God, you get stupider every day.

10   TONY: Luke, knock it off.

11   LUKE: I'll knock it off when he starts behaving like a man.

12   STEVEN: So I don't go to a stinking party or get drunk with

13   you and your jock friends. That means I'm not a man?

14   You're pathetic.

15   TONY: Steven, listen, this isn't the first time you dogged us

16   about going out. Why won't you do normal things?

17   STEVEN: Like what?

18   TONY: Well, for example, when was the last time you went to

19   a football game?

20   STEVEN: I didn't realize it was abnormal to be bored by

21   football. Sorry. And I do go.

22   TONY: When?

23   STEVEN: When I don't have band rehearsal.

24   LUKE: Ha! Band rehearsal. You and that band. A bunch of

25   artsy fartsy weirdos who hide behind their guitars and

26   keyboards at every party and dance they go to.

27   STEVEN: We get paid pretty well to play, you know.

28   LUKE: Big claim to fame — you pick up a quick hundred

29   dollars to split between the four of you. When you gonna

30   come out from behind that guitar and face the real world?

31   STEVEN: And, please, Luke, tell me, what is the real world?

32   LUKE: High school.

33   STEVEN: Well, if you think high school is the real world then,

34   thanks, but no thanks. You can keep it. A bunch of

35   pseudo-macho males denigrating everyone who doesn't

1   conform to their personal standards of identification.

2   LUKE: Who talks like that? Tony, tell me, who talks like that?

3   Steven, who do you know that talks like that besides you?

4   STEVEN: Like what?

5   LUKE: "Pseudo-macho," "denigrating," and all that crap?

6   Who are you trying to impress? Me?

7   STEVEN: Just because I'm familiar with the English language...

8   LUKE: Drop the superior show, my young friend, and let's

9   remember who got the 1350 on the SAT, OK?

10   STEVEN: Fluke.

11   LUKE: Fluke *this*, little brother.

12   STEVEN: Both of you just get out of my room.

13   TONY: Why should we?

14   STEVEN: Because I'm asking you to.

15   TONY: We're not leaving until this is settled.

16   STEVEN: What's there to settle? I'm different from you, so

17   I'm weird. I'm different than most guys at school, so I'm

18   not part of that "crowd" you hang with. I like music, I

19   can paint, I can't catch a football, so I'm a fag. Hey,

20   whatever, guys.

21   LUKE: You said it, not us.

22   STEVEN: Is that what you're afraid of, Luke? That I might be

23   gay? Would it be such a horrible thing?

24   LUKE: It would sure as hell explain a few things.

25   TONY: Why are we even discussing this? You're not gay. You're

26   not. *(STEVEN looks at him blankly.)* Are you?

27   STEVEN: Would it make a difference?

28   LUKE: It sure would with me. I don't want to be seen having a

29   brother who's a fairy.

30   TONY: Come on, Steven. This is a stupid conversation. It's not

31   worth the trouble of even talking about it.

32   STEVEN: I think it is. Luke is clearly upset at the idea. *(He*

33   *saunters over to LUKE and speaks in a lispy voice.)* What's

34   the matter, Lukey? Afraid I'll come on to one of your jock

35   friends? You know, that Jonathan is really cute. Had my

1   eye on him a long time. Blond hair, grey-green eyes, big
2   bulging biceps. Hmmm-hmmm.
3   LUKE: *(Grabbing him)* Shut up!
4   TONY: This isn't funny, Steven.
5   STEVEN: *(Squealing like a girl)* Ooohhh, let go!
6   LUKE: *(Stunned at the squeal, releases STEVEN.)* God, you are
7   such a creep. You make me sick.
8   STEVEN: *(Still lispy voice)* Do I? Why? Because your brother
9   might be more different than you thought?
10   LUKE: You wouldn't be my brother anymore, that's for
11   damn sure.
12   STEVEN: *(Normal voice)* You're not serious.
13   LUKE: Serious as death.
14   STEVEN: What an ass. Tony, can you believe what you're
15   hearing?
16   TONY: *(Quietly)* Yeah.
17   STEVEN: Did you ever hear anything so stupid and narrow-
18   minded?
19   TONY: I don't know.
20   STEVEN: *(Disbelieving)* You, too?
21   TONY: We shouldn't even be talking about this. I mean, come
22   on. It's a stupid discussion about nothing.
23   STEVEN: Would it be that big a deal, really?
24   LUKE: If my brother was a gay boy? Hell, yes.
25   STEVEN: Tony?
26   TONY: You want me to lie?
27   STEVEN: I can't believe this. So, you're saying that if I told you
28   right now that I was gay, you'd disown me?
29   LUKE: *(Looking him straight in the eye)* First, I'd beat the
30   living crap out of you, and then I'd disown you.
31   TONY: Come on, Luke. Don't get stupid.
32   LUKE: You think I'm stupid? How do you think Dad would
33   react, Steven?
34   STEVEN: I don't know.
35   LUKE: Get real. He'd hate it. He'd hate you. That's a fact and

1   you know it.

2   STEVEN: No, I don't.

3   TONY: I think you're going a little far.

4   LUKE: Like hell I am. What does Dad always call us? His men.

5   From the time we were little, we've been his men. Steve,

6   buddy, don't you know what a disappointment you are to

7   Dad by not playing football or soccer or baseball? How do

8   you think it makes him feel to see his youngest son pick

9   up a guitar or dance around on a stage rather than be on

10   a field?

11   STEVEN: He says he's proud of me. Last year, after the

12   musical, he said he was proud of me.

13   LUKE: That's what he said to your face. Tony, remember what

14   he said at intermission?

15   TONY: Shut up, Luke.

16   LUKE: Tell him what Dad said.

17   STEVEN: Tell me, Tony.

18   TONY: It was no big deal. He was making a joke.

19   STEVEN: If it's no big deal, then tell me.

20   LUKE: I'll tell him...

21   TONY: He said, "Remember when we used to go watch Steven

22   play Little League baseball? Now we go to watch my son

23   in a dress."

24   STEVEN: The show was *Sugar.* I had to wear a dress. That was

25   the point of the play.

26   LUKE: You didn't have to be in it. No one forced you.

27   STEVEN: No, no one forced me. But I did it and I loved it and

28   I was damn good.

29   TONY: No one said you weren't.

30   STEVEN: Hell, we got a standing ovation.

31   LUKE: Yeah, and I led it. I stood up to walk out and everyone else

32   thought I was standing to applaud. I was so embarrassed to

33   see my brother up on the school stage looking better in a

34   dress than most of the girls, I had to leave.

35   STEVEN: Tony? You felt the same way?

1   TONY: It was a little hard to face our friends.

2   STEVEN: Well, look at your friends. A bunch of drunken
3   slobs. Yeah, that's a group of people I want to impress.

4   TONY: You just don't get it, do you? Maybe Luke has a point.
5   Maybe you are more different than you want to admit.

6   STEVEN: I'm not afraid to admit anything. But I am certainly
7   not going to sit here and be judged by two people who
8   obviously have no respect for what I care about.

9   LUKE: So, are you gay or what?

10 STEVEN: What?!

11 LUKE: Answer the question.

12 STEVEN: I'm not answering anything. You've made up your
13   mind about who I am, so fine. No matter what I say or
14   what I do, because it's not exactly like you two and Dad,
15   then I'm a fag. Hey, if that's the way it is, then that's the
16   way it is.

17 TONY: Steven, you're not gay.

18 STEVEN: Maybe I am and maybe I'm not. Or maybe you have
19   your own doubts about your masculinity. Could that be
20   why you have to play the big jock all the time? Especially
21   you, Luke. You know, I've always wondered why it was
22   you spent so much time in the locker room. First one in
23   and last one out. All those sweaty guys, showering,
24   steaming, you seem to really enjoy that.

25 LUKE: It's not gonna work, Steve, so give it up.

26 STEVEN: What's not gonna work?

27 LUKE: Your little innuendos. I *know* who I am. I think you
28   have some doubts.

29 TONY: I have to agree with Luke, Steve.

30 STEVEN: I have no doubts about who I am. And I don't have
31   to justify what I do or what I like or who I like to a pair of
32   close-minded, conformist, insensitive assholes like you.
33   Now, get the hell out of my room!

34 LUKE: Fine. But listen to what I'm saying and trust that I
35   mean it. Whatever it is you decide you are, you do it after

1   you leave this house and you never share it with the
2   family. I never want to know one way or the other. You
3   got that?
4 STEVEN: You will never understand anything that isn't
5   exactly like you. You won't even try.
6 LUKE: Nope. *(He exits.)*
7 TONY: Don't pay any attention to him. He may have gotten a
8   1350 on the SATs, but he's not a bright boy.
9 STEVEN: Did Dad really make that comment about the dress
10   at the musical?
11 TONY: It doesn't matter.
12 STEVEN: Did he?
13 TONY: Yeah. But he was kidding. It was a joke. He laughed.
14   And he loved the show.
15 STEVEN: I guess.
16 TONY: Don't worry about it.
17 STEVEN: Yeah.
18 TONY: You OK?
19 STEVEN: Yeah.
20 TONY: OK. Well, I guess I'll just go now.
21 STEVEN: Tony...
22 TONY: Yeah?
23 STEVEN: Would it make a difference to you?
24 TONY: *(After a moment)* I don't know, Steve. But you are my
25   brother, no matter what.
26 STEVEN: Thanks.
27 TONY: Play your guitar, kid. I like to leave my bedroom door
28   open and listen to you. *(He leaves as STEVEN plays softly*
29   *and sadly.)*
30
31
32
33
34
35

Grandpa

(Scene for two women)

1   *(KATHY, and her younger sister JULIA, discuss the*
2   *problems of growing old.)*

3   **KATHY:** Julia, is Mom home yet?

4   **JULIA:** Not yet.

5   **KATHY:** Did she say when she'd get home?

6   **JULIA:** Nope.

7   **KATHY:** No note? Nothing?

8   **JULIA:** No note, nothing.

9   **KATHY:** Great. Have you started dinner?

10   **JULIA:** No. Was I supposed to? No one told me.

11   **KATHY:** Just once it would be really nice if you did something
12   without having to be told.

13   **JULIA:** *(A beat)* Yeah. OK.

14   **KATHY:** You are something else, you know that?

15   **JULIA:** Uh-huh.

16   **KATHY:** Did you at least clean up the dishes?

17   **JULIA:** No, Kathy, I didn't clean up the dishes.

18   **KATHY:** Good grief, you are beyond belief.

19   **JULIA:** I'll do it, OK. I was planning on doing it later. Not
20   everything has to be done on some mythical schedule
21   you've decided on.

22   **KATHY:** Well, please, don't put yourself out. God forbid that
23   you might actually help out around here without having
24   to be told.

25   **JULIA:** I said I'd do the dishes later.

26   **KATHY:** Forget it. Don't bother getting up, please. I'll take
27   care of them. God knows I take care of everything else
28   around here lately.

29   **JULIA:** Martyr mode. Good.

30   **KATHY:** And just what does that mean?

31   **JULIA:** Just that you're at your happiest when you can do it
32   all and make sure that everyone knows you're the one
33   doing it.

34   **KATHY:** Someone's got to follow through around here. It's for
35   sure that it isn't going to be you.

1   JULIA: Fine! You want them done now, I'll do them now!
2   KATHY: Good! Do it!
3   JULIA: What are you going to do?
4   KATHY: Well, I can assume that there is still laundry sitting
5   on the washer that has yet to be done, the carpets need
6   vacuuming, and dinner needs to be started. So, I guess
7   that will keep me busy, unless, of course, you managed to
8   take care of at least some of the chores. *(No response from*
9   *JULIA)* Just as I thought.
10 JULIA: I said I'd take care of the dishes for you.
11 KATHY: What do you mean for me? You are not doing me any
12   favors, you know. Why, all of a sudden, are you thinking
13   you're doing the dishes for me?
14 JULIA: Forget it. *(She begins to exit.)*
15 KATHY: And clean up your crap from the room.
16 JULIA: Why don't you quit telling me what to do?
17 KATHY: Because if I don't, nothing gets done. And Mom
18   doesn't need to come home to the house looking like this.
19 JULIA: She won't even notice.
20 KATHY: The hell she won't.
21 JULIA: She doesn't notice anything anymore. We could not
22   even be here and she wouldn't miss us.
23 KATHY: Is there anyone more selfish than you?
24 JULIA: Well, she wouldn't.
25 KATHY: For once in your life, quit thinking about yourself and
26   think about someone else. Mom is going through enough
27   right now without you throwing your attitude at her.
28 JULIA: I don't know why she has to be at the hospital all
29   the time.
30 KATHY: Because her father is dying. Grandpa is dying.
31 JULIA: He's been dying. Why doesn't he get it over with?
32 KATHY: *(A beat)* I can't believe you just said that.
33 JULIA: *(Quietly)* Well, I did. And I mean it, too.
34 KATHY: No, you don't.
35 JULIA: Yeah, I do.

1   KATHY: I have never in my life heard anything so awful come

2   out of your mouth. I've known you to be unbelievably

3   selfish, self-centered and wrapped up completely in your

4   own needs, but this is out of control, even for you.

5   JULIA: Why is it selfish? Honestly, why? He's going to die

6   anyway, isn't he?

7   KATHY: He's had bad times before and pulled out of them.

8   He'll pull out of this one, too.

9   JULIA: Take off the rose-colored glasses, Kathy. Join the real

10   world. Grandpa is dying. He's been sick for a long time

11   and dying a little bit more everyday. He's done nothing

12   but get worse.

13   KATHY: He has good days.

14   JULIA: When? When was the last good day he had? A year ago?

15   Maybe longer?

16   KATHY: How would you know? When was the last time you

17   went to see him?

18   JULIA: What's the point? He doesn't even remember who we

19   are anymore.

20   KATHY: He does too remember. Maybe not our names, but he

21   knows we are family. His eyes light up when we come in

22   the room and hug him.

23   JULIA: His eyes light up whenever anyone walks in the room

24   and gives him a hug. He's a friendly guy. However,

25   whether you want to accept this or not, he has no idea

26   who we are.

27   KATHY: You are so cold.

28   JULIA: No, I'm not. I'm realistic. I've watched Grandpa

29   shuffling around, looking at all of us without really

30   knowing who we are, unable to complete a coherent

31   sentence, and then I watch Mom get sadder and sadder.

32   There is no point to this.

33   KATHY: God does not give us more than we can bear. What

34   does not kill us makes us stronger.

35   JULIA: Well, I feel better now. Clichés sure can brighten up a

1   cloudy day. Why don't you tell Mom that when she comes
2   back from watching her father deteriorate into an empty
3   shell.
4   KATHY: *(She looks at JULIA for a moment, then quietly)* I have
5   things to take care of.
6   JULIA: Yes, do what you always do. Walk away from reality.
7   For God's sake, don't face what is happening.
8   KATHY: Oh, be like you? Wish Grandpa right into his grave.
9   JULIA: If you had any compassion, you would.
10   KATHY: Compassion? You talk to me about compassion? Who
11   makes sure things are taken care of? Not you. Who tries
12   to comfort Mom when she feels down about everything
13   that is going on? Not you. Who goes to visit Grandpa in
14   the home? Not you.
15   JULIA: I do my share, dammit. Maybe I'm not as vigilant
16   about dusting the nooks and crannies of this house, but
17   I do help out. And I do try to talk to Mom, but it's hard.
18   KATHY: And visiting Grandpa? What about that?
19   JULIA: I can't. I just can't. It's too hard to take.
20   KATHY: Ah, here we go. Now we're getting down to it. It's too
21   hard to take for poor little Julia. Never mind the times he
22   was there for you. Let's just forget all about that. Forget
23   about the Disneyland trips, the donut hunts, dancing at
24   parties, basketball games. Let's just forget everything we
25   ever did with Grandpa and take care of ourselves. That is
26   just so typical of you.
27   JULIA: You don't get it, do you? Don't you see that those are the
28   memories I want to keep alive? I want to remember that
29   man that I loved, that I looked up to, the way he was then,
30   not the way he is right now. I don't even know this person.
31   KATHY: Well, you better try to know him while there's still
32   time to do so.
33   JULIA: That's just it. There is no time anymore. I didn't tell
34   you this, but I did go down to see him about a month ago.
35   KATHY: Why didn't you tell me?

1   VICKY: I didn't want to talk about it.

2   KATHY: Why? When did you go?

3   VICKY: I went down to the home after school one day to see

4   how he was. It had been a long time, at least a couple

5   months since I'd been down there. You know what he

6   did? He looked at me. No, he looked through me.

7   KATHY: Did you tell him who you were?

8   JULIA: I shouldn't have to tell him who I am. I'm his

9   granddaughter for God's sake. He was in the delivery

10   room when I was born. He should know who I am.

11   KATHY: He can't help what is happening to him.

12   JULIA: I know that, I'm not stupid. But it gets worse. I stayed

13   for just a few minutes, and then he said he had to use the

14   bathroom.

15   KATHY: Did you call someone to help him?

16   VICKY: It was too late. He had gone already.

17   KATHY: He did?

18   JULIA: *(Quietly)* Yeah. He looked so helpless, so confused.

19   Then, when the nurse came to get him, he smiled at her

20   like he smiled at me and he just walked away with her.

21   He just walked right away with her as if he had

22   completely forgotten I was there. And he probably had.

23   KATHY: I didn't know he had lost control over his bodily

24   functions.

25   JULIA: Why don't you just say it? He peed all over himself.

26   That's what he did. And I had to stand there and watch.

27   Just watch and there was nothing, not a damned thing I

28   could do. And if it makes me feel this bad, how do you

29   think it makes Mom feel? It's her father, the man who

30   raised her, who taught her about life, who changed her

31   diapers. Now she has to change his. It's just not fair.

32   KATHY: No, it's not, but it has to be dealt with.

33   JULIA: Why? Why does it have to be dealt with like this? Do

34   you remember Duchess?

35   KATHY: The cat?

1   JULIA: Yeah, the cat. We had that cat forever.

2   KATHY: Mom and Dad got it before we were born.

3   JULIA: Didn't you love that cat?

4   KATHY: Yes, of course I loved Duchess.

5   JULIA: More than you love Grandpa?

6   KATHY: Two different things.

7   JULIA: OK, fine, but let's say Grandpa was drowning and so

8   was Duchess the cat. Who would you try to save?

9   KATHY: Grandpa, of course.

10   JULIA: So you love Grandpa more, OK?

11   KATHY: OK. What's your point?

12   JULIA: How did Duchess die?

13   KATHY: We had to put her to sleep because she...

14   JULIA: She what?

15   KATHY: Nothing...

16   JULIA: Don't say nothing, Kath. We had to put her to sleep

17   because...

18   KATHY: *(A beat)* Because she was...I don't want to talk about

19   this. I really don't.

20   JULIA: We need to talk about this. We put her to sleep because

21   she got old and sick and "lost control of her bodily

22   functions."

23   KATHY: Duchess was a cat.

24   JULIA: So why is a cat allowed to die with dignity? Why is it

25   humans are forced to live a life of degradation?

26   KATHY: I said I don't want to talk about this.

27   JULIA: How do you think Grandpa would feel if he knew what

28   was going on? Do you think he'd want to live like this?

29   KATHY: I don't know.

30   JULIA: The hell you don't. Would you want to? I know I

31   wouldn't.

32   KATHY: You can't say that.

33   JULIA: Yes, I can. Let me tell you right now, sister dear, that if

34   I should come down with this horrible humiliating

35   disease called Alzheimer's, put a pillow over my face and

1   call it a day. There is no way I'd want to live like that.

2   KATHY: So what do you suggest we do? Smother Grandpa in his

3   bed? Take him out of the home on a trip and leave him on

4   some city street? Maybe throw him in front of an oncoming

5   car. What do you think would be the humane thing?

6   JULIA: I have no idea. But I do know that this is all wrong.

7   There is nothing right about what he is going through.

8   KATHY: Well, just thank God our family has enough money to

9   provide a good place for him to live comfortably.

10   JULIA: And that's another thing. What about people that

11   don't have that kind of money? You didn't go with Mom

12   when she had to finally make the decsion to put Grandpa

13   in a home. You should have seen some of those places.

14   Dirty, disgusting, smelly. Some of those old people were

15   walking around with clothes that reeked of urine. Not

16   nearly enough caretakers for the patients. How do you

17   think those families feel who can't afford what we can in

18   the way of care and they have to visit their mothers,

19   fathers, grandparents? And what about us? Grandpa is

20   only sixty-seven years old. He could live for another ten

21   years like this, lingering in and out of consciousness,

22   that dull vacant look in his eyes when he does come

23   around. Financially this could wipe Mom and Dad out.

24   KATHY; And what if it's hereditary?

25   JULIA: What?

26   KATHY: I'll be honest with you. I have thought about all of

27   this. Maybe that's why I'm so obsessed with doing

28   everything around here. It's my way of not thinking.

29   JULIA: Thinking about what?

30   KATHY: About that this might be genetic. Mom could get it,

31   then it could be us. Then what?

32   JULIA: It won't happen. They'll have a cure by then.

33   KATHY: You think? I don't. There's tons of money going for

34   cancer and for AIDS. But what about Alzheimer's? You

35   never hear anything about it. There won't be a cure if

1   there is no research.

2   JULIA: There will be. There has to be.

3   KATHY: I'm scared all the time. Everytime Mom comes in a
4   room and forgets why she came in, it scares me. When
5   she misplaces something, it freaks me out.

6   JULIA: Everyone does that. We all forget things. It doesn't
7   mean...

8   KATHY: I know it doesn't. Intellectually I know. But
9   emotionally...

10   JULIA: I thought you were the strong one through all this.

11   KATHY: That's what I try to be. I keep thinking that if I keep
12   busy, if I keep things going here in the house and make
13   sure that everyone is taken care of, then maybe nothing
14   will happen.

15   JULIA: You can't stop things from happening. Like I said,
16   Grandpa is going to die. He should get it over with. And I
17   don't mean that in a cruel way.

18   KATHY: I know.

19   JULIA: He should have dropped dead of a heart attack five
20   years ago on the basketball court. That's how he would
21   have liked to go. That's a memory I would have loved.
22   Grandpa's last days being who he was – active, fun, and
23   doing what he loved. Not this shell of a man who just
24   stares into space.

25   KATHY: It would have been better. Better than this.

26   JULIA: Yeah. *(They sit for a moment in silence.)* I'll do the dishes.

27   KATHY: OK. Mom should be home pretty soon.

28   JULIA: I think we should talk to her.

29   KATHY: Why?

30   JULIA: Because she probably feels exactly what we are
31   feeling, but is too guilty to talk about it. She needs to be
32   able to talk about it. Like we just did.

33   KATHY: Yeah. I guess so. Yeah. God, this sucks.

34   JULIA: It does, doesn't it?

35

On My Own

(Monolog for one man)

1   *(NATHAN talks about his relationship with his father.)*
2   NATHAN: Today was the one-year anniversary of my dad's
3   funeral. I loved him and I know he loved me. But I hardly
4   knew him. I've been pretty much on my own since I was
5   a kid. Not that I'm that old now, but I'm sure not a kid.
6   Dad was a lawyer. Criminal defense. He was pretty good,
7   I guess, because people were always calling the house to
8   get him to defend their low-life relatives from some
9   crime they were accused of. I couldn't understand how
10   he could do that, but he said if we are to have justice in
11   this country, then everyone has a right to a fair trial, both
12   the guilty and the innocent. Yeah, I guess, but how fair is
13   it when someone who is guilty walks free? He could
14   never explain that part of it.
15   Dad was one of a kind. Really smart, star athlete,
16   school government, everything I want to be, but doubt I
17   will. My mom says I'm just as good as Dad. I guess so.
18   Everything I know about my dad I learned from my
19   mom. Dad was never one for talking. At least not to me.
20   Oh, I always knew he loved me, but I wasn't sure he liked
21   me. I feel kind of strange saying that, but that's how I
22   feel. He was always in court or a law library or meeting
23   with a client or something. I honestly don't remember
24   him coming to a game or a concert or anything I did at
25   school. Mom was always telling me that he wanted to be
26   there, but work and all...I don't know. It always seemed to
27   me that if he really wanted to be there, he would. Mom
28   came. Not all the time, but most of the time. She works,
29   too. She teaches, so she's off during summer and
30   vacations, but she always has papers to grade and tests to
31   prepare and all that kind of stuff. She used to get mad at
32   Dad sometimes, though, when I had a football game or
33   something and he couldn't be there. One time I
34   remember them arguing about it. But you know, it was
35   really no big deal to me. I was used to him not being

1   there, so you know, so what, right?
2   There was a time when I was little that I used to get
3   mad about looking up into the stands at, say a Little
4   League game. He, of course, would tell me he would try
5   to be there. Like a jerk, I'd spend the whole game
6   watching the stands instead of the field hoping I'd see
7   him. One time – and this is really dumb – one time I
8   looked up and I thought I saw him. I was so excited, you
9   know? Then it was my turn to bat and I knew I was going
10   to hit that ball out of the park. So I lined myself up at the
11   plate, took my practice swing, and then waited. The
12   pitcher threw the ball. Strike one! I wasn't worried. I
13   knew I was going to nail the ball. The pitch and strike
14   two! OK, now I started to get worried. I looked up and
15   saw those sunglasses he always wore, shining there. I
16   thought I heard him call out to me. I was so happy. I had
17   to hit the ball out of the park for him, make him proud,
18   make him want to come to all my games. I looked at that
19   pitcher and inside I dared him to try to strike me out.
20   Dared him! Well, he looked me dead in the eyes, wound
21   up, and fired a pitch so fast all it was to me was a blur. I
22   swung hard and heard a big "crack." I'll be damned if I
23   didn't hit the hell out of the ball. I stood there and
24   watched it go into this beautiful high arch and fly like it
25   had wings right out of the field. I figured the only one
26   more surprised and happier than me at that moment
27   would be my dad. The coach yelled at me to circle the
28   bases, and I did. You'll never have a greater feeling than
29   running the bases after a home run! As I rounded third
30   to home, I looked up and waved at my dad. But he wasn't
31   watching me. He had taken off his glasses to clean them.
32   That's when I saw it wasn't him. The only home run I
33   ever hit and he wasn't there. He had promised that for
34   sure, this time, he'd be at that game. But he wasn't. No
35   one from my family was there. When I got home, Mom

1   told me she had a student conference, and when Dad
2   finally got home, at about nine o'clock, he apologized
3   and said he had to meet with a client being held for
4   murder. So it goes, right? I didn't even tell them about
5   the home run. I mean, what was the point? It wasn't like
6   they had planned to not be there just to make me
7   unhappy. They both had to be at their jobs and that was
8   important. That was the last year I played Little League.
9   It just didn't seem all that important, you know?
10   I spent a lot of time playing really cool video games
11   when I was home alone. I wasn't allowed to go outside or
12   have anyone in the house if my parents weren't home.
13   That was OK...I mean I understood it because they
14   wanted me safe. But it was kind of a drag to have to come
15   straight home from school and stay in the house until
16   they got home. Everyone else would hang out at school
17   and play basketball or something, but I had to be home.
18   After awhile, though, that got old, so I started staying at
19   school and hanging out with my friends until right
20   before Mom would get home. See, school was out at two
21   forty-five for me, and three o'clock for her. But she always
22   had to stay after and work with kids. She was the on-site
23   math tutor, so she never really left school until about
24   four-thirty, then it took her about half an hour to get
25   home, so I was on my own until five o'clock. I didn't do
26   bad things. Can't do much bad in less than two hours.
27   One time, though, my friends and I went to the mall and
28   got our ears pierced. Neither of my parents noticed for
29   about two weeks. By the time they did I just told them
30   that I had done it months earlier and all the kids did it.
31   What was cool was my dad noticed it first about eleven
32   o'clock at night. He said something, then my mom came
33   in and they had a discussion about it, but it was late and
34   they were tired, so by the time they were done talking
35   about it, they just told me it was my ear and I could do

1   what I thought was right. The funny thing is, though, I
2   was kind of hoping they'd get mad and tell me to take it
3   out. My friend Glenn got his ear pierced that same day.
4   He got home and his parents noticed it right away. Boy,
5   were they mad. They grounded him for a week. I gave
6   him a hard time about it. But you know what? I was
7   jealous. I wished my parents had paid enough attention
8   to get mad at me about it. Hell, I wish they had just
9   noticed that I had done it.
10 Jeez, it sounds like my parents are bad. But they're not.
11 Or weren't. Whoa, Dad's gone. Wow. Dad has passed
12 away. He's not with us. Dad is dead. Anyway you say it
13 doesn't make it better. He died really dumb, too. Not even
14 something that he'd be proud he died of, like saving
15 someone from a burning building or pushing a child out
16 from in front of an oncoming car. Nope, he died choking.
17 He was running late to an appointment with one of his
18 criminals and stopped to get some chicken at a fast-food
19 place. He did what he always did, which was eat in the
20 car in the parking lot. He would never eat while he drove,
21 because he said it was unsafe and he didn't want to cause
22 an accident. But he choked on a chicken bone. And he
23 was alone. Alone with a bone. I can almost guarantee you
24 that his last thought wasn't of me and my mom. His last
25 thought had to be, "Well, this is dumb."
26 So, Dad's been gone a year. In some ways I miss him. I
27 don't miss money, because he had a great insurance plan
28 and savings and stuff, so financially we're OK. And it's
29 not like I miss him at the dinner table, because he was
30 never really there for dinner. In fact, I don't think I can
31 really remember ever sitting down and having dinner at
32 an appointed time. Glenn gets in huge trouble if he's not
33 home by six-thirty. Dinner is on the table and everyone
34 better be there or there is hell to pay. I eat there a lot. It's
35 gotten to be a kind of joke with his family, because they

1   just automatically set a place for me at dinner. No, it's
2   weird. I don't really miss my dad, because I was used to
3   him never being around. When he was alive I could
4   always have the hope that he would show up for a game.
5   I could dream that some day he would put me first over
6   one of the criminals and actually show up for something
7   when he said he'd show up. When Dad was alive I could
8   hope that some day, maybe some day, we'd sit down and
9   have that father/son stuff going on. I figured it would
10   probably happen when I grew up. But now it won't. I'm
11   going to grow up and Dad won't be there. You know
12   what's really scary, though? I can't remember what he
13   looked like. Oh, we have pictures and stuff. But I look at
14   them and I can't remember him being there in person. I
15   look at those pictures and see a stranger.

16   I tried to talk to my mom about it all. Not easy. At first
17   she was pretty shook up. But after a few months, she
18   settled back into her job. She's working on her Ph.D. in
19   education because she wants to be an administrator. I
20   guess that's good. Whatever, huh? She's dating. My mom
21   has dates. More dates than me. What does that tell you
22   about my social life. What kind of bothers me, though,
23   is that she can suddenly find the time to date, be-
24   cause before she and Dad couldn't find the time to be
25   together as a family. Does anyone see the irony in that
26   besides me?

27   So, like I said, I'm pretty much on my own. I have a car
28   now, and Mom has let up on the be-home-no-one-in-the-
29   house stuff, which is good, because I wasn't doing it
30   anyway. She never knew, so so what. So, I go to school,
31   keep my grades up, and hang out at the mall with my
32   friends and do sports. I think I've done a helluva job
33   raising myself. I'm a good kid. But I feel lonely
34   sometimes. I go home to our big old house and hear my
35   footsteps echo on the stairs. I make myself dinner and do

my homework. I'd play with a dog if I had one, but Dad was allergic and Mom said dogs were dirty, so I lost out there. I go out with my friends and try to beat Mom home. She has late-night classes at the university. And don't forget her dates. Anyway, I take care of me.

It hasn't been all that easy being on my own, especially when you look around and see friends that have parents who are there for everything. But other people have it worse than me. At least my parents stayed together and tried to make sure I had everything I needed. But it would have been nice to have them there, you know?

So, Dad's been dead a year. I don't miss him, really. He wasn't around that much to miss. And I'm not mad at him. I mean, he worked hard to be a good lawyer and he had to work hard to stay at the top. What I miss is the idea of a dad. I go to the cemetery sometimes. To be honest, I go to the cemetery more than Mom. I sit by his grave and talk to him, tell him what's going on in my life. I ask for his advice and if I'm really quiet and listen really hard, sometimes I feel he answers me. I didn't feel this close to him when he was alive. One thing I remember, though, is when I'd be asleep. I was usually in bed before he got home from work. I remember hearing him open the door and I'd open my eyes so that he'd know I was still awake. I could see the light beam through the crack of the door. Then Dad would come in and sit on the bed for a minute and pat my back and mess up my hair. He'd say, "Good night, Natty." He never called me Nathan unless he was mad; it was always Natty. Hey, that was one really good thing about him not being around when my friends were around – they couldn't hear him call me Natty. Anyway, I remember his hand on my hair, and his good night and I would pat his leg and tell him I loved him. And now, sometimes when I talk to him at the cemetery, the wind will blow, just a

1   little bit. Just enough to mess up my hair. If I really
2   listen, I can hear him say, "Good night, Natty." I put my
3   hand on his grave and I whisper, "I love you, Dad"
4
5
6
7
8
9
10
11
12
13
14
15
16
17
18
19
20
21
22
23
24
25
26
27
28
29
30
31
32
33
34
35

Perspectives on
Growing Up

College Life

Always Late

Where You Going?

Fresh Starts

Old Habits

College Life

(Scene for two men)

1   *(BERT enters RYAN's room as he prepares to head off to*
2   *college.)*
3   **BERT:** What are you doing?
4   **RYAN:** Finishing my packing.
5   **BERT:** Already? You don't leave for a couple days.
6   **RYAN:** Yeah, I know. I'm just excited. Who would have
7   thought that I'd actually get accepted to Stanford on a
8   full ride?
9   **BERT:** *(Under his breath)* Not me...
10   **RYAN:** What?
11   **BERT:** Nothing. Whatcha taking?
12   **RYAN:** Pretty much everything.
13   **BERT:** *(Looking at a picture in a frame)* This, too?
14   **RYAN:** Hell, yes. I think this is my favorite picture of us.
15   **BERT:** Us with Santa Claus?
16   **RYAN:** Yeah. Stupid, huh?
17   **BERT:** A little embarrassing, I would think.
18   **RYAN:** Yeah? Just because we're sitting on Santa's lap?
19   **BERT:** Ryan, we took that picture this year for your mom. No
20   one else was ever supposed to see it.
21   **RYAN:** I know. But I like it. It says something to me.
22   **BERT:** Me, too. It says, "Look at the morons on Santa's lap.
23   They need to grow up."
24   **RYAN:** Hey, now. We've taken our picture together with Santa
25   every year since we were in third grade. My mom's still
26   got copies of all of them.
27   **BERT:** Great. Just when you think it's safe to go out in public,
28   your mom whips out those damn pictures.
29   **RYAN:** You know you love it.
30   **BERT:** Maybe. You taking your photo albums?
31   **RYAN:** Not all of them. Just this one I put together. *(He pulls it*
32   *out.)* Look at this. You're in almost every picture with me.
33   **BERT:** How many vacations did our families take together?
34   **RYAN:** All of them. Look at this one. Remember body skiing at
35   Lake Havasu?

1   BERT: *(Laughing)* **Our parents thought we were idiots, just**
2   **hanging on to the ski rope and getting dragged behind**
3   **the jet ski.**
4   RYAN: **God, that hurt!**
5   BERT: **But it was fun, huh?**
6   RYAN: **Yeah. Hey, remember this night?**
7   BERT: **Vegas! Who are those girls?**
8   RYAN: **I have no idea. I just remember your sister bet us ten**
9   **dollars we couldn't get dates by midnight, so we hooked**
10 **up with these two.**
11 BERT: **Yours isn't bad. Jeez, though, look at the Alpo-**
12 **muncher I'm with.**
13 RYAN: **Didn't matter what she looked like. It mattered that we**
14 **got our money out of your sister for winning the bet.**
15 BERT: **What's this one?**
16 RYAN: **Our first day of school in third grade the summer after**
17 **we met. And this one is our first day in junior high. And**
18 **this is our first day of high school.**
19 BERT: **You save everything on film?**
20 RYAN: **My mom does, you know that.**
21 BERT: **We've been friends a long time.**
22 RYAN: **Forever.**
23 BERT: **Too bad you won't have a picture of us together on our**
24 **first day of college.**
25 RYAN: **Yeah.**
26 BERT: **Yeah. You excited?**
27 RYAN: **Oh, yeah. Nervous, excited, bunch of stuff. This is a big**
28 **move for me, you know.**
29 BERT: **Yeah, I know. Me, too.**
30 RYAN: **College is a serious business.**
31 BERT: **Yeah, it is. So is moving away.**
32 RYAN: **I can't believe it. Two more days and I'm shaking the**
33 **dust of this ratty little town off my shoes. College life,**
34 **here I come.**
35 BERT: **You're really lucky, you know. Not everyone is lucky**

1	enough to get a full scholarship to Stanford.
2	RYAN: I worked hard for that scholarship, Bert. You know
3	that.
4	BERT: Yeah, I know. Throwing that ball must have really
5	taken it out of you.
6	RYAN: It wasn't just for baseball, you know. It was for my
7	grades, too.
8	BERT: Yeah. That 3.5 was a tough one to get. And that 1100
9	you scored on the SATs was pretty impressive.
10	RYAN: It was 1150, thank you very much. You know, you need
11	to get past this.
12	BERT: You're right. Of course you're right. You're the big
13	college guy and I'm just the little J.C. guy. What do I
14	know? Never mind the fact that I had a 3.8 and scored
15	1200 on my SAT. However, I didn't play varsity ball. I was
16	busy doing community service and working with ASB
17	and active in my church. I see where I screwed up. What
18	a fool I was.
19	RYAN: Sarcasm isn't your style, you know.
20	BERT: Yeah, well, you let me know how they handle these
21	things when you get back from Stanford during winter
22	break. I'll be where I've been for the last two years when
23	I'm not at school: working at Wal-Mart.
24	RYAN: Jeez, Bert, move on. Get over yourself. So I'm going to
25	Stanford on an athletic scholarship. What do you want
26	me to do, turn it down?
27	BERT: It's just not fair. Dammit, I worked hard, too!
28	RYAN: You got accepted, you could have gone.
29	BERT: No, because I can't afford it.
30	RYAN: Well, I'm sorry. OK, I'm sorry. It's not fair. Life isn't fair.
31	BERT: Well, the least you could do is be a little sympathetic.
32	RYAN: I am sympathetic. But it's not the focus of my world.
33	I'm the one going away from my friends and family...
34	BERT: Shaking the dust of this ratty little town off your shoes
35	was the way you put it.

1 RYAN: OK, so I was a little more explicit than I meant to be.
2 BERT: You seem to forget that I'm still going to be stuck in
3   this ratty little town.
4 RYAN: Not forever.
5 BERT: Yeah, right.
6 RYAN: Only if you choose to be.
7 BERT: Come on, Ryan, get real. I will never be able to afford a
8   place like Stanford. I won't get a scholarship. I won't get
9   the best education I am capable of. I'm stuck.
10 RYAN: You're not stuck. You've got plenty of opportunities.
11   You just have to take advantage of them.
12 BERT: Oh yeah, great. I'm sure every major corporation in the
13   country will be hunting down a graduate from the J.C.
14 RYAN: So you go to the J.C. for two years, then you finish up at
15   a four-year.
16 BERT: State college is all I will ever be able to afford. And I'll
17   be lucky if I can manage that.
18 RYAN: You are so negative.
19 BERT: That's so easy for you to say from your perch on top of
20   the world. Free education, free books, room and board.
21 RYAN: I have to work, you know.
22 BERT: Please. No doubt some lightweight job like handing
23   out towels for the girls' gymnastic program.
24 RYAN: You know, you'd think, as my best friend, you'd be a
25   little happy for me.
26 BERT: You'd think.
27 RYAN: What do you want me to do? Turn it down? "Oh, sorry,
28   Stanford, but my best friend Bert can't make it here, so I
29   am going to give up my chance of a lifetime and turn
30   down the scholarship. Thanks anyway, maybe next year."
31 BERT: You could at least show a little empathy for me.
32 RYAN: Empathy? For what?
33 BERT: For the fact that I'm stuck here, dammit. Your life is
34   taking off and I'm locked in this crappy town for the rest
35   of eternity.

191

1   **RYAN:** You're pathetic. Everything is such a negative with you.

2   **BERT:** It is not.

3   **RYAN:** Like hell it isn't.

4   **BERT:** Example?

5   **RAN:** OK. Like when we were going to try out for the school

6   musical. We get there and wait around for hours. When

7   it's finally our turn to sing, you chicken out.

8   **BERT:** I can't sing.

9   **RYAN:** Neither can I. That was the whole point. It was exciting

10   to give something a try that we were pretty sure we'd

11   fail at.

12   **BERT:** I still don't see how failure is exciting.

13   **RYAN:** Bert, it isn't the failure that's exciting. It's cheating

14   failure that is the rush. Trying something you know you

15   only have a small chance of succeeding at and then

16   winning. That's what it's all about.

17   **BERT:** Yeah, but you made the show.

18   **RYAN:** You probably would have, too, if you'd stayed and

19   given it a shot. But you left.

20   **BERT:** I didn't want to be laughed at.

21   **RYAN:** Don't you see? I knew I couldn't sing, so I wasn't

22   expecting anything. I got up there and just sang really

23   loud. That way I laughed *with* them, they didn't laugh *at*

24   me. So it was fun. And being in the show was fun.

25   **BERT:** It looked like fun.

26   **RYAN:** And you could have done it, too. Every guy that tried

27   out made the show. And all the girls were hot!

28   **BERT:** I know. I'm an idiot. I was just scared.

29   **RYAN:** You can't live your life in fear, my friend.

30   **BERT:** It's not fear. It's caution. I play it safe.

31   **RYAN:** You don't play at all. Like going to the J.C. Where are

32   you going?

33   **BERT:** You know as well as I do that I'm going to Hanlon.

34   **RYAN:** Right. You and everyone else from school who's not

35   going to a four-year. Why don't you go to Avery?

1   BERT: Because I won't know anyone there.

2   RYAN: Exactly! It would be a whole new start. You could be a
3   whole new person. So you can't afford to go to a four-year.
4   Accept it and make the best of it.

5   BERT: *(Annoyed)* Yeah, yeah, life give you a lemon, make
6   lemonade.

7   RYAN: Right! Your problem is that you spend days examining
8   the damn lemon and by the time you get around to
9   making the lemonade, the thing has lost its zing!

10   BERT: Oh, I should be like you and just use the lemon
11   without examining it?

12   RYAN: Yeah!

13   BERT: OK, and let's say I get a bad lemon, and don't examine
14   it closely and someone has used a hypodermic needle
15   and injected some poison in the lemon. So, if I were you
16   and didn't look carefully at the peel of the lemon, I'd die.
17   What kind of sense does that make?

18   RYAN: *(Looking at him a moment in stunned silence)* Forget it,
19   you're hopeless.

20   BERT: Tell me I'm wrong.

21   RYAN: Never mind.

22   BERT: You know I'm right. I will live a long time because I'm
23   careful.

24   RYAN: You will live a long time because you don't take action.
25   You can't get too hurt sitting in a rocking chair waiting
26   for life to happen.

27   BERT: I don't wait for life to happen. I don't sit around. I'm
28   careful; I think things through.

29   RYAN: Yeah, while you're sitting there, thinking things
30   through, there's a lot of living going on.

31   BERT: Hey, live a clean life, live a long life.

32   RYAN: Right. Avoid fat and sugar, exercise regularly, die any-
33   way. Listen to me. It goes back to this scholarship thing.

34   BERT: Which isn't fair, which you know as well as I do.

35   RYAN: Maybe, but there's more to it than that. I figured back

1   in our freshman year that I had one shot at getting into a
2   good school and that was through baseball. So I jumped
3   on it. You know how hard I worked, and it was a long
4   shot, but it came through. The funny thing is, you had
5   more talent than I ever did. I don't know why you didn't
6   stick with it.
7 BERT: Because I thought I'd be able to do it on grades and
8   SATs and that stuff. Stupid me.
9 RYAN: Yeah, but you know that more scholarships are given
10   for athletes. And you were good.
11 BERT: It was too much of a risk. I had to be sure that I was
12   doing what I thought was right.
13 RYAN: And so...?
14 BERT: So, you're going to Stanford and I'm going to Hanlon.
15 RYAN: Yeah.
16 BERT: Yeah.
17 RYAN: Bert, we're given only one chance on this earth. Don't
18   be afraid to try.
19 BERT: Try what?
20 RYAN: Everything. You're like one of the smartest people I
21   know. You just hold back too much.
22 BERT: Yeah?
23 RYAN: Yeah. So, you're going to the J.C. Go to Avery, not
24   Hanlon. If you go to Hanlon with everyone from high
25   school you'll never change.
26 BERT: Who says I want to change? Maybe I'm happy the way I
27   am. You ever think of that?
28 RYAN: Tell me, what are you going to major in?
29 BERT: Business with a minor in political science.
30 RYAN: Why?
31 BERT: Because that way I can get a good job with a good
32   corporation and make a decent living. Why else?
33 RYAN: But you hate that kind of stuff. I don't understand you.
34   You are so intelligent and so talented, but you are going
35   to be satisfied with a mediocre life.

1   BERT: Mediocre?

2   RYAN: *Good* job, *good* corporation, *decent* living. Come on,

3   you deserve more than average in your life.

4   BERT: What's the deal? You're majoring in exactly the same

5   thing I am. Why is it all right for you and not me?

6   RYAN: Because I have a passion for business and law. And I

7   don't plan on working for a decent corporation. My plan

8   is to own my own corporation, specializing in social

9   ecology. Set your sights high or you'll never get off the

10   ground. What do you have a passion for?

11   BERT: I don't know.

12   RYAN: I do. Kids and music. You're terrific at both.

13   BERT: I hate performing, you know that. I play the piano

14   for me.

15   RYAN: And for those kids you work with at the community

16   center.

17   BERT: It calmed them down. They liked it.

18   RYAN: So do something with it.

19   BERT: Like what? Travel from center to center playing piano

20   for hyper kids?

21   RYAN: No, moron. Music therapy.

22   BERT: Huh?

23   RYAN: Music therapy. It's a whole field of psychology where

24   they use music as a means to get through to kids who've

25   been abused or something. It's perfect for you.

26   BERT: I've never even heard of it.

27   RYAN: I heard about it on *Donahue* or *Oprah* or something.

28   There's a whole field of it opening up. Not a lot, but some

29   schools are offering it as a major.

30   BERT: Like where?

31   RYAN: *I don't know!* God, you want me to lay it all out for you?

32   BERT: I need details.

33   RYAN: Try finding them out for yourself, man. Investigate.

34   BERT: Music therapy, huh?

35   RYAN: Yeah.

1   BERT: I guess I could look into it.
2   RYAN: Yeah, you could.
3   BERT: I don't know, though. How secure is it?
4   RYAN: Don't make me hurt you, Bert.
5   BERT: OK, OK, I'll look into it.
6   RYAN: Try it. Try living without the safety net for at least a
7   while. You're an old man in an eighteen-year-old's body.
8   BERT: All right, your point is made. I'll look into it.
9   RYAN: And maybe, when we're both out of school, you'll have
10   your own psychology practice and need a good business
11   lawyer.
12 BERT: Who, you?
13 RYAN: Of course, me.
14 BERT: Nah, I think I'll want someone a little more stable.
15 RYAN: *(Laughingly)* Shut up.
16 BERT: I'll be here to take you to the airport.
17 RYAN: Thanks.
18 BERT: And don't forget, December 19, noon, the mall,
19   Santa's lap.
20 RYAN: Thought I wouldn't?
21 BERT: See ya.
22 RYAN: See ya.
23
24
25
26
27
28
29
30
31
32
33
34
35

Always Late

(Scene for one man and one woman)

1   *(JANICE and BOBBY are a long-time couple. They are at*
2   *JANICE's home preparing to go to a wedding rehearsal*
3   *dinner. BOBBY waits impatiently.)*
4   **BOBBY:** *(He is mumbling and pacing, becoming increasingly*
5   *agitated each time he glances at his watch.)* **Sometime**
6   **today would be really nice. I don't know, someone tells**
7   **me to be someplace at a specific time, I'm there! Just this**
8   **weird little quirk of mine called consideration.** *(Calling*
9   *off)* **Janice! Today, please!**
10   **JANICE:** *(Calling back)* **You know when you rush me it only**
11   **makes me nervous which makes me go slower, so stop**
12   **yelling.**
13   **BOBBY: Maybe I wouldn't have to yell if things were done**
14   **properly.**
15   **JANICE:** *(Entering, brushing her hair)* **Oh, for heaven's sake.**
16   **It's only six-thirty. We've plenty of time before we're late.**
17   **BOBBY: Plenty of time? Plenty of time. OK, the invitation**
18   **clearly states that the rehearsal dinner starts at seven**
19   **o'clock. I figure it takes us twenty minutes to drive there,**
20   **five minutes to find a parking space, two minutes to walk**
21   **in, a minute to find the right room. That gives us a leeway**
22   **of only three minutes. That's cutting it pretty damn close.**
23   **JANICE: We really need to have you taken in for a colon check.**
24   **BOBBY: What does that mean?**
25   **JANICE: You are just so anal.** *(She puts on her lipstick.)* **Do you**
26   **like this color?**
27   **BOBBY: It's fine, terrific. You look great. Get in the car.**
28   **JANICE: I don't know. I think it might be too pinkish with this**
29   **dress.**
30   **BOBBY: It's perfect. You look beautiful. Get in the car.**
31   **JANICE: These shoes are tight.**
32   **BOBBY: You can take them off under the table at dinner.**
33   **JANICE: How rude!**
34   **BOBBY: No one will know the difference.**
35   **JANICE: But people will be eating. I can't do that. Give me**

1	one minute to find my other tan shoes. I know they are
2	around here somewhere.
3	BOBBY: You're going to be sitting most of the night. You don't
4	need to wear comfortable shoes.
5	JANICE: But I have to walk in. You want me to walk in looking
6	like I'm in pain?
7	BOBBY: If they hurt so much, why did you buy them?
8	JANICE: Bobby, please, look at these shoes. They are so cute
9	and they go great with that sea green dress I bought for
10	the wedding.
11	BOBBY: So, these shoes you're changing out of now you plan
12	on wearing tomorrow to the wedding?
13	JANICE: Yes.
14	BOBBY: They hurt too much to wear at dinner tonight, but
15	they'll be fine tomorrow, is that what you're saying?
16	JANICE: Silly. Tomorrow at the wedding I can take them off
17	in the pews. And then at the reception there will be
18	dancing and everyone takes their shoes off for that. Good
19	grief, don't you know anything?
20	BOBBY: I know we're late.
21	JANICE: Well, don't just stand there, help me look.
22	BOBBY: Listen, we've narrowed our leeway time by a full
23	minute. As it is, if there is any traffic at all we'll be late.
24	JANICE: So we're a few seconds late. *(She goes off to find her*
25	*shoes.)* We'll be fine. Bobby, be a sweetheart and see if my
26	shoes are under that cushion in the corner.
27	BOBBY: You know, if you'd put things away properly, you
28	wouldn't have to look for them because you'd know
29	where they were. They'd be *away!*
30	JANICE: Uh-huh. I found them!
31	BOBBY: Where?
32	JANICE: In the tub. *(Entering, shoes in hand)*
33	BOBBY: In the tub? Why were they...? Never mind, I don't
34	want to know.
35	JANICE: Just two minutes and I'll be ready. You watch, Megan

1   and Charlie won't get there till about quarter after seven.

2 BOBBY: Megan and Charlie can be late. It's their rehearsal
3   dinner. They have the right to be late. We're just invited
4   guests.

5 JANICE: Please explain to me why we were invited to this
6   dinner. We're not in the wedding.

7 BOBBY: Because my band is playing for the reception.
8   Charlie and Megan just want us to feel like we're a part of
9   the whole thing.

10 JANICE: OK. I think it's silly, but OK. *(She sits to change her*
11   *shoes.)* I mean, why would his parents want...what? What
12   are you looking at?

13 BOBBY: What are you doing?

14 JANICE: I'm changing my shoes.

15 BOBBY: And you can't do that in the car?

16 JANICE: If I did, you know I'd end up leaving the other ones
17   in your back seat, I'd forget that I did, I'd leave them, next
18   time I wanted them I couldn't find them because they
19   wouldn't be in the house, they'd be in your car and then
20   I'd really be late. So, no, I can't change them in the car.

21 BOBBY: We are so late!

22 JANICE: Calm down, we have to wait for George.

23 BOBBY: Why do we have to wait for George?

24 JANICE: Because he needs a ride.

25 BOBBY: I thought he was going to meet us there.

26 JANICE: Didn't I tell you?

27 BOBBY: Tell me what?

28 JANICE: George called this afternoon. I told you, you just
29   don't listen.

30 BOBBY: You didn't tell me.

31 JANICE: I could have sworn I told you. Hmmm. Oh well, he
32   called.

33 BOBBY: ...and said?

34 JANICE: That he needed a ride. I just told you that.

35 BOBBY: But why?

1   JANICE: I don't know. Do I look like Robert Shapiro? I didn't
2   cross-examine the man. He said he needed a ride, I said OK.
3   BOBBY: Did you tell him we'd be leaving at six-thirty?
4   JANICE: I told him sometime between six-thirty and seven.
5   BOBBY: Which means he won't get here until quarter after
6   seven. We are going to be so late. This is just un-freaking-
7   believable. This is rude. Forget taking your shoes off
8   under the table. This late is just plain rude. Rude!
9   JANICE: It's not my fault he needs a ride. He's your lead
10   singer, not mine.
11   BOBBY: He is *such* a loser! He needs a ride because he doesn't
12   want to spend his own gas money. I have never met
13   anyone like your brother.
14   JANICE: Hey, at least he has a job now. That, in and of itself, is
15   a small miracle.
16   BOBBY: Yeah, great job. Waiter at Spoons. Now there is a
17   strong career move at twenty-three.
18   JANICE: He's finding himself.
19   BOBBY: Hello! This isn't 1968. Our parents *found* themselves.
20   We don't have time for that luxury. The world is moving
21   too damn fast to take time to *find* yourself. He should
22   have gone to college and prepared himself for the real
23   world. You know, the real problem is that he will just
24   never grow up.
25   JANICE: Why should he when Mom and Dad let him live at
26   home?
27   BOBBY: He is so frustrating to talk to. So much talent and he
28   throws it away. A voice like his and he is content to just
29   sing in a pick-up band.
30   JANICE: Don't sell your band short. You guys are really good.
31   BOBBY: Yeah, we're really good. But bottom line is all we are
32   is a pick-up band. We're all going to have real jobs that
33   are careers. Ron is going to be a teacher, I'm heading
34   towards architecture, Stan is going for his divinity
35   degree to be a minister.

1   JANICE: Don't forget about your drummer.

2   BOBBY: OK, so Steve is a postal employee.

3   JANICE: Uh-huh. One step closer to that Uzi...

4   BOBBY: Stop it, not all of them are crazy.

5   JANICE: Have you noticed since he's been working there his
6   eyes have gotten just a tad wild?

7   BOBBY: At least he's got a full-time job. George works part-
8   time as a waiter. He lives at home, he drives the same
9   rotting car he drove in high school, and now we are going
10   to be late because of him. Dammit, this whole night
11   is doomed.

12   JANICE: Oh, please. So we walk in late, big deal.

13   BOBBY: Doesn't it bother you at all that we're late?

14   JANICE: No. Not really.

15   BOBBY: It's such an impolite thing to do.

16   JANICE: Everyone knows that Janice and Bobby are always
17   late. It's like our trademark.

18   BOBBY: No, it's like your trademark. I hate being late. I was
19   never late till I started going out with you. I was always
20   on time. You know, all through high school I never got a
21   tardy. I never once had to serve detention for tardies.

22   JANICE: It wasn't so bad. I met a lot of interesting people in
23   detention.

24   BOBBY: How nice for you.

25   JANICE: Hmmm, I don't know. Maybe the other shoes look
26   better. What do you think?

27   BOBBY: I think you look great. Let's go.

28   JANICE: I can't go yet. I need to change purses.

29   BOBBY: You need to what?!

30   JANICE: Well, you certainly can't expect me to carry this
31   purse with these shoes can you?

32   BOBBY: I guess not. What was I thinking? How cruel of me to
33   even suggest it.

34   JANICE: Very funny. Ha, ha. *(She begins to switch the contents*
35   *of one purse to the other by dumping everything out and*

1	*just sweeping it all into the other one with a flat hand,*
2	*careful of her nails.)*
3	BOBBY: You need help with that?
4	JANICE: If you would.
5	BOBBY: Do you really need everything that's in there?
6	JANICE: Every single thing.
7	BOBBY: Women's purses are a mystery. What is all that?
8	JANICE: Just stuff that I need.
9	BOBBY: Like what? *(He sifts through a couple things.)*
10	JANICE: You know, woman's stuff, like tampons and other
11	things.
12	BOBBY: *(Immediately drops whatever it was he was holding.)*
13	You do it.
14	JANICE: OK, that should do it. What about George?
15	BOBBY: What about him?
16	JANICE: What's he going to do? Show up here to find a dark
17	house, no car in the driveway and his best friend has left
18	him high and dry.
19	BOBBY: Yes.
20	JANICE: You are so mean.
21	BOBBY: Be that as it may. You told him between six-thirty and
22	seven, and he's not here. It's now ten minutes to seven. It
23	is no longer *between,* it is now *almost.* We're leaving. As
24	it is we will probably walk in as they are serving the
25	salads. We are going to completely miss the mingling
26	part of the evening.
27	JANICE: Mingling?
28	BOBBY: You know, where you mingle, talk, connect. Nope, we
29	are going to totally miss that part and have to jump right
30	in on the croutons.
31	JANICE: So what are we going to do about George?
32	BOBBY: Leave him a note. A *short* note. I'll write it. Where's
33	something to write with and something to write on?
34	JANICE: There's probably something in my purse. *(She hands*
35	*it to him.)*

1   BOBBY: You're not going to look? I have to?

2   JANICE: You mean dig around in there? I just did my nails.

3   BOBBY: You don't have a pad of paper and a pen next to the
4   phone like most normal people? *(She gives him a wan*
5   *smile.)* No, I didn't think so. *(He digs into purse and finds*
6   *a piece of paper and a sliver of a pencil.)* This will do.

7   JANICE: See, aren't you glad I didn't clean my purse out? We
8   wouldn't have had that paper to write a note.

9   BOBBY: Yeah, great.

10   JANICE: What is that paper, before you write on it?

11   BOBBY: Gum wrapper.

12   JANICE: Oh, wait, is there anything written on it?

13   BOBBY: No. Should there be?

14   JANICE: Sometimes I put phone numbers and stuff...*well!* I
15   can't help it, I'm not as organized as you. Sorry.

16   BOBBY: Why do I sometimes feel like I'm Ricky and you're
17   Lucy? OK, here's the note. Do you have some tape or
18   something so I can stick it to the door?

19   JANICE: There might be some in the bathroom.

20   BOBBY: The bathroom?

21   JANICE: Sometimes I have to hem a skirt real quick so I
22   use...never mind. *(She grabs a blouse from the chair and*
23   *pulls a safety pin out of the front of it.)* Here, use this.

24   BOBBY: Why do you have a safety pin in this blouse?

25   JANICE: I lost the button and I needed to wear it to work
26   today, so I just pinned it. Here, just bend it open and it
27   will be like a tack. Stick it on the front door and we're set.

28   BOBBY: You are unbelievable.

29   JANICE: I manage.

30   BOBBY: I don't know how. One of these days they will find
31   you strewn out, taped, safety pinned and shoeless lost on
32   some city street starving because you forgot your money
33   in your other purse. Are we finally ready?

34   JANICE: I've been ready. You're the one that had to go on and
35   on about George and then the note thing and everything.

1   You're the reason we're going to be late.
2   BOBBY: I...you...the shoes...Just get in the car.
3   JANICE: OK.
4   BOBBY: Do you have the directions?
5   JANICE: *(A pause while she thinks)* **Ummm...yes!**
6   BOBBY: Prove it.
7   JANICE: *(She digs around in her dress bodice, then triumph-*
8   *antly pulls out a note with the directions.)* **A-ha! Here they are.**
9   BOBBY: You put them in there?
10   JANICE: That way I knew I wouldn't lose them! Pretty clever,
11   huh? And I bet you thought I'd lost them.
12   BOBBY: The thought never crossed my mind. Let's go. And
13   when we get back, we need to have a long talk about
14   priorities.
15   JANICE: Mine or yours?
16   BOBBY: Ours.
17   JANICE: Ours, huh? Sounds interesting. I didn't know we had
18   reached the "ours" stage.
19   BOBBY: Long time ago.
20   JANICE: Was I late?
21   BOBBY: *(Affectionately)* **You're an idiot. You know I love you.**
22   JANICE: In spite of my flaws?
23   BOBBY: Probably because of them.
24   JANICE: *(Going to him)* **You sweet thing.**
25   BOBBY: *(Hugging her)* **Thank you. Come on, we need to get**
26   going.
27   JANICE: We're late already. What's a few minutes more going
28   to matter? *(She kisses him.)*
29   BOBBY: Don't do this... *(He kisses her back.)*
30   JANICE: Don't do what? *(She kisses him again.)*
31   BOBBY: This. *(He kisses her.)*
32   JANICE: But it's so much fun.
33   BOBBY: We're going to be really late.
34   JANICE: Yeah. But when they ask us why, won't this be a
35   really good reason?

1   BOBBY: Yeah, I guess so...

2   JANICE: Oh look, there's that nice couch just waiting for us

3   over there.

4   BOBBY: No, Janice, now come on. *(She kisses him.)* Oh, what

5   the hell.

6

7

8

9

10

11

12

13

14

15

16

17

18

19

20

21

22

23

24

25

26

27

28

29

30

31

32

33

34

35

Where You Going?

(Scene for one man and one woman)

1   (*MEGAN and CHARLIE are both in their early twenties.*
2   *MEGAN is sitting by herself, looking up at the stars.*
3   *CHARLIE enters, sees her and approaches.*)
4   **CHARLIE:** Hey.
5   **MEGAN:** Hey.
6   **CHARLIE:** You been here long?
7   **MEGAN:** Not very.
8   **CHARLIE:** I looked for you at the party but you were gone.
9   **MEGAN:** And here I am.
10   **CHARLIE:** You always come to the parking lot at night.
11   **MEGAN:** It's quiet. I can think.
12   **CHARLIE:** About what?
13   **MEGAN:** Nothing. Everything. Stuff.
14   **CHARLIE:** You OK?
15   **MEGAN:** Yeah, I'm OK.
16   **CHARLIE:** You thinking about leaving again?
17   **MEGAN:** Uh-huh.
18   **CHARLIE:** Where you going?
19   **MEGAN:** (*Looking up at him, then looking away*) **Barcelona.**
20   **CHARLIE:** (*A familiar reply*) **Oh.**
21   **MEGAN:** Why is it I always feel like I am in the middle of a bad
22   Stephen Sondheim musical when you're around?
23   **CHARLIE:** 'Cause nothing's gonna harm you...
24   **MEGAN:** (*Joining in with him*) **"Not while I'm around..."** Yeah,
25   great.
26   **CHARLIE:** I'll do my best.
27   **MEGAN:** Well, thanks, Charlie. Thanks.
28   **CHARLIE:** No problem. So, what are you doing here?
29   **MEGAN:** I don't know. Waiting.
30   **CHARLIE:** For what?
31   **MEGAN:** I don't know, just waiting I guess.
32   **CHARLIE:** Can't just wait, Megan. Can't just do the generic
33   wait. Gotta be waiting for something.
34   **MEGAN:** (*She begins to sing "Something's Coming" from* West
35   Side Story.) **Something's coming, I don't know what it is...**

1   CHARLIE: OK, enough with quoting musicals. What's the
2   deal with you? Why are you sitting in the middle of the
3   parking lot at ten o'clock at night?
4   MEGAN: It's as good a place as any.
5   CHARLIE: Yeah, I guess it is. Mind if I wait with you?
6   MEGAN: *(No anger, just matter-of-factly)* **Char, you can do**
7   **anything you damn well please.**
8   CHARLIE: **Then I will. I'll just sit myself down here and wait**
9   **with you.**
10 MEGAN: *(Quietly)* **Great.**
11 CHARLIE: *(After a moment)* **This is...good. Waiting...for some-**
12   **thing. It's a good thing.**
13 MEGAN: **If you're going to be here, Char, you have to shut up.**
14 CHARLIE: **I can do that. Shutting up.**
15 MEGAN: Good.
16 CHARLIE: **Yep. If there's one thing I pride myself on, it's my**
17   **ability to know when to speak and when not to speak.**
18 MEGAN: **Uh-huh.**
19 CHARLIE: **Yessiree. I can tell you don't want to talk...**
20 MEGAN: *(Overlapping)* **That's right...**
21 CHARLIE: **...and I don't want to push it.**
22 MEGAN: *(Overlapping)* **...and I appreciate that...**
23 CHARLIE: **...because when you're ready to talk, I know you**
24   **will...** *(He looks for some kind of response)* **...and I'll be**
25   **here, right here, waiting...just waiting...** *(Still no response)*
26   **...yes, indeed, just wait...**
27 MEGAN: **Charlie, please.**
28 CHARLIE: **OK.** *(They sit for a moment.)*
29 MEGAN: **You don't have to stay, you know.**
30 CHARLIE: **I know.**
31 MEGAN: **Good** *(Quietly)* **I'm OK, Charlie. Really I am.**
32 CHARLIE: **I know you are.**
33 MEGAN: **Good.**
34 CHARLIE: *(After a moment)* **You leaving?**
35 MEGAN: **Thinking about it.**

1   CHARLIE: Where you going?

2   MEGAN: Hell, I don't know. Somewhere different.

3   CHARLIE: What's wrong with here?

4   MEGAN: Same old same old.

5   CHARLIE: You gotta stop running some day, you know.

6   MEGAN: I'm not running, Char. I'm just leaving. Look
7   around you. Every day is exactly like the one that came
8   before and the one that's coming after. You get up, you
9   go to work, you go home, you go to bed. Everybody in
10   this place has the same goal...mediocrity. There's more
11   to life. I know there is. There's got to be more. I couldn't
12   stand it if there weren't.

13   CHARLIE: You've been like this since we were kids. You
14   always talk about leaving, but you never do.

15   MEGAN: Maybe this time I will.

16   CHARLIE: Maybe...but why?

17   MEGAN: Dammit, Charlie, quit asking me questions I have no
18   answers to. I just know that I've got to leave. I feel like the
19   walls are closing in on me.

20   CHARLIE: Do you have a plan?

21   MEGAN: My plan is to sit right here and wait.

22   CHARLIE: And a good plan it is. Come on, Megan, let's
23   go home.

24   MEGAN: Why are you here?

25   CHARLIE: For you.

26   MEGAN: You're a good friend.

27   CHARLIE: The best.

28   MEGAN: My best. *(A deep sigh)* God, Char, life sucks, doesn't it?

29   CHARLIE: No...

30   MEGAN: No?

31   CHARLIE: Moments suck. Life, overall, is pretty good.

32   MEGAN: Then why do I feel so bad all the time?

33   CHARLIE: *(He shrugs; this is old territory.)* Don't know.

34   MEGAN: You really like how your life is?

35   CHARLIE: Yeah. I'm doing OK. I'm getting married...

1   MEGAN: She's very nice.

2   CHARLIE: I think so. I've started a great job...

3   MEGAN: Your future is pretty much mapped out. You're set.

4   CHARLIE: There's always room for surprises. For new things.

5   MEGAN: Is there?

6   CHARLIE: I'll make room.

7   MEGAN: I feel like nothing new is ever going to happen to
8   me if I don't leave now. Nothing will ever change for me.
9   I'll be stuck here in this rotten little town for the rest of
10   my life.

11   CHARLIE: With those of us who love you.

12   MEGAN: Those who love me.

13   CHARLIE: Yes.

14   MEGAN: Is that enough?

15   CHARLIE: *(Looking at her)* Maybe not.

16   MEGAN: Maybe not. I used to think it was.

17   CHARLIE: I did too.

18   MEGAN: I don't know anymore.

19   CHARLIE: Then go.

20   MEGAN: What?

21   CHARLIE: *(Frustrated)* Quit talking about it and go. You're
22   always talking about it, but you're never doing it. If
23   you're going to go, do it now.

24   MEGAN: I will.

25   CHARLIE: When?

26   MEGAN: Soon.

27   CHARLIE: When? When is soon? It's been soon for a long
28   time. Soon has come and gone. Now it's later.

29   MEGAN: Is it?

30   CHARLIE: You know what your problem is? You spend way
31   too much time focused on you. I think the worst thing
32   you ever did was go to therapy.

33   MEGAN: Dr. Webster helped me get in touch with my inner
34   child.

35   CHARLIE: I think your inner child needs a good smack on the

1   butt. You've got far too much time on your hands. You sit

2   around looking at life and waiting for things to happen.

3   Well, honey, have you noticed that all you do is wait?

4   Wait and complain. You know what your main problem

5   is? It's not this town. It's not the people. It's you. You're

6   the problem.

7   MEGAN: You have no idea what I'm talking about. You hear

8   the words, but you don't listen to the context or the

9   meaning.

10   CHARLIE: The context and meaning? The context and

11   meaning are that you are just doing what you always do,

12   which is reacting to the moment instead of thinking...

13   MEGAN: Are you saying I'm incapable of thinking?

14   CHARLIE: No. If you would listen, you'd hear what I was saying.

15   MEGAN: OK, I'm listening.

16   CHARLIE: What I'm saying is that you are scared of your own

17   destiny. You are afraid of taking that next step along the

18   road to being an adult. If you leave, you can do what you

19   do best, which is to avoid facing being an adult. If you

20   leave, you can remain a little girl, which for you, it seems

21   to me, is where you want to stay. Grow up, Meg.

22   MEGAN: Go to hell.

23   CHARLIE: You go to hell. At least it would be a step in *some*

24   direction. I swear, I have just about had it with you.

25   Inner child, getting in touch with your feelings,

26   emotional dumping. Why don't you try growing up?

27   There's a novel concept.

28   MEGAN: You have no idea what I'm going through.

29   CHARLIE: Oh my God. Who has been there for you through

30   every stinking crisis since we were in high school? Who

31   was there for you when your parents got divorced? When

32   you needed help for anything? Moving furniture,

33   opening bottles, holding you when you wanted to cry?

34   Being there. Me, dammit. That's who. Me.

35   MEGAN: I know. I know. You are my best friend. I don't know

1   what I would do without you. I don't want to lose you.

2   CHARLIE: *(Softly)* What's wrong, Megan? Don't you love me?

3   MEGAN: You know I do. Sitting out here in this parking lot
4   alone, I knew you would come to me. I knew you'd try to
5   make me feel better. It's just that I worry that something
6   is missing, and it's me.

7   CHARLIE: *(Hugging her)* I know, I know. It's a big step. But
8   you know it's the right one...don't you? Right now,
9   holding you, I know that there's nowhere else I want to
10   be. Right now, at this moment, I am happy. It's good, the
11   two of us.

12   MEGAN: What if we're not always happy? I was sitting there
13   tonight, listening to your father make that toast. "To
14   Megan and Charlie, a long and happy life." Charlie,
15   honey, what if it's not happy? What if it's just long and
16   nothing else? I'm so scared.

17   CHARLIE: Me, too.

18   MEGAN: You are?

19   CHARLIE: Yes. But, I know that as long as we're together it
20   will be OK. We are each other's strength and support. We
21   are each other's best friend. I look into your eyes and I
22   see my future.

23   MEGAN: You do?

24   CHARLIE: Uh-huh. I see it so clearly. And it's so good.

25   MEGAN; Hold me close, Charlie.

26   CHARLIE: *(He does.)* It's pretty out here. You know, you never
27   really get a chance to appreciate the beauty of a parking
28   lot until it's empty. The symmetry of the lines marking
29   each stall. The contrast of the white paint against the
30   black of the asphalt. It really is a beautiful thing.

31   MEGAN: You are so weird.

32   CHARLIE: No, not really.

33   MEGAN: Who else but you could see a parking lot as a
34   beautiful thing? It's just a bare space.

35   CHARLIE: We all see what we want to see.

1   **MEGAN:** Yeah, I guess we do. *(She looks up at him and smiles.)*
2   I guess it's in the way you look at it.
3   **CHARLIE:** Yeah. *(He holds her close.)*
4   **MEGAN:** Yeah.
5
6
7
8
9
10
11
12
13
14
15
16
17
18
19
20
21
22
23
24
25
26
27
28
29
30
31
32
33
34
35

Fresh Starts

(Scene for three women)

1   *(CARRIE, DONNA and SHARON are in the very nice foyer*
2   *outside a bathroom during the wedding reception of*
3   *MEGAN and CHARLIE. CARRIE enters in her bridesmaid*
4   *dress followed shortly by DONNA and SHARON.)*
5   CARRIE: *(She enters dressed in a voluminous bright*
6   *bridesmaid gown, capped with a large hat. She is obviously*
7   *relieved that the room is empty.)* **Hello, anyone in here?**
8   *(No response)* **Thank God. What a lousy day.** *(She reaches*
9   *in her bra and pulls out a lone cigarette.)* **I'm just going to**
10   **smell it, I'm not going to smoke it. Mmmm.** *(Seeing*
11   *herself in the full-length mirror)* **Well, aren't you pretty?**
12   **Here alone? Still stuck in that crummy job with no hope**
13   **for a future? Still going out with Bert, the original**
14   **nowhere man?** *(Fidgeting with the hapless pile of fabric*
15   *that is her dress.)* **There's got to be a bathroom in here**
16   **somewhere. I knew I should have said no to Megan about**
17   **being in her stinking wedding. Look at me. God, this is**
18   **depressing.**
19   SHARON: *(Entering)* **Is this the bathroom?**
20   CARRIE: **Do you see a toilet? No, you don't.**
21   SHARON: **Wow! Take a look at this!** *(Calling off)* **Donna, come**
22   **look at this.**
23   DONNA: *(Entering)* **At what? Oh, wow! Is this the bathroom?**
24   SHARON: **Do you see a toilet?**
25   CARRIE: **Sharon, come on, help me with this damn dress.**
26   DONNA: *(Looking around approvingly)* **What is this?**
27   CARRIE: **It must be a dressing room or something.**
28   SHARON: **Pretty snazzy. Where's the john?**
29   CARRIE: **I would guess it's down this little hallway.** *(She takes*
30   *another sniff of the cigarette.)*
31   SHARON: **Are you planning on smoking that cigarette?**
32   CARRIE: **I quit, remember?**
33   SHARON: **Then why do you have it?**
34   CARRIE: **Old habits die hard. I just want to smell it.**
35   DONNA: **If you're not going to smoke it, can I?**

1   SHARON: Hey! We all agreed that smoking was unhealthy
2   and we weren't going to do it anymore.
3   DONNA: Oh, easy for you. You never smoked.
4   SHARON: Why you two ever started smoking in the first place
5   I will never understand.
6   CARRIE: 'Cause I was *coool*. I was a *coool* person in high
7   school. Donna, who was *coooler* than us?
8   DONNA: Nobody, Carrie, nobody.
9   SHARON: I was *coool* too, remember? I didn't smoke.
10 CARRIE: Lucky you. You were about the only one who didn't.
11   Pretty much all of us smoked then. Speaking of all of
12   us, is there anyone at this wedding we haven't known
13   since birth?
14 DONNA: No kidding. I was hoping for at least one fresh face
15   among the crowd.
16 SHARON: I suppose there are a few. Charlie has to have more
17   friends than just Megan, you know. He must have met
18   *someone* in college who's new. I saw one or two really
19   cute guys.
20 CARRIE: Where? I saw no one.
21 SHARON: Hard to see much of anything from behind that
22   hat. Take the damn thing off.
23 CARRIE: What? It's not me? Aren't I fetching in this lovely
24   ensemble?
25 DONNA: More like you should *be* fetching. Why does every
26   bride feel it necessary to surround herself with
27   hideously dressed friends? Is it like a last laugh as she
28   rides off into the sunset with her Prince Charming?
29   However, take a look at the castle she's inheriting.
30 CARRIE: Tell me how Megan managed to land herself a rich
31   guy like Charlie? Not only does he have money, but he's
32   great looking, sweet and darling, and his parents adore
33   her almost as much as he does.
34 SHARON: I am pretty impressed that they agreed to have the
35   wedding at their home. You *ever* seen a house like this?

1   CARRIE: How many bathrooms do you know that have a lobby?

2   DONNA: How many houses do you know that have this many

3   bathrooms?

4   CARRIE: Look at this — a couch, a table, this little footstool is

5   too much. A full-length mirror. Hey, look, there's a bunch

6   of little cosmetics and stuff.

7   SHARON: Cool *(She picks up several and dumps them in her*

8   *purse.)*

9   CARRIE: What are you doing?

10 SHARON: Well, these are obviously here for the guests. I'm a

11   guest, this is my color. You know how hard it is to find

12   this color? Or this one? I knew I brought my big purse for

13   a reason.

14 CARRIE: Good lord, you have no shame, do you?

15 SHARON: Nope. Donna, do you like this lipstick for you?

16 DONNA: Yeah, put it in your purse.

17 SHARON: All righty. *(She does.)* OK, I have to pee. Can I go first?

18 CARRIE: You go ahead. It will take me an hour to pull myself

19   out of this dress.

20 SHARON: No problem. I'll help you when I get back.

21 CARRIE: We'll wait here. I need a short rest after dragging

22   this mound of organdy and lace around. And these

23   matching shoes are a nightmare of pain. *(She kicks off*

24   *her shoes and looks around.)*

25 DONNA: This is a damn nice layout. Is it as classy in there as

26   it is out here?

27 SHARON: Wait till you see this bathroom! Are you sure people

28   actually pee here, or is it for show? I'm afraid to sit down

29   on the seat; it looks like it's made of pearl.

30 CARRIE: Hover over it.

31 SHARON: I'm afraid I'll splash. Pink pearl toilet seat. It's

32   gorgeous.

33 CARRIE: Just go, OK? Quit admiring and go.

34 DONNA: There are others of us who need to use the

35   facilities...

1   SHARON: I'm going. Wow, wait till you see this toilet paper.
2   I've never felt such soft toilet paper. They must have it
3   custom made. You can't get this at Safeway.
4   CARRIE: *(Stretching out on the divan)* Imagine, a waiting
5   room for a toilet. Pretty ritzy. *(She leans over and*
6   *examines a small table next to the divan.)* Chocolates!
7   SHARON: What?
8   CARRIE: Chocolates! There are Godiva chocolates on this
9   table. I've died and gone to bathroom heaven. Donna,
10   you want some?
11 DONNA: We're talking chocolate here. When have I ever
12   turned down chocolate?
13 SHARON: You're going to eat in a bathroom?
14 CARRIE: What?
15 SHARON: Eating in a bathroom. That's kinda disgusting,
16   don't you think?
17 CARRIE: In the first place, Godiva chocolates eaten anywhere
18   are never disgusting. In the second place, this isn't a
19   bathroom, it's an antechamber... *(A toilet flushes.)*
20 SHARON: *(Re-entering)* A what?
21 CARRIE: An antechamber. Poor people, like us, have bathrooms.
22   Rich people, on the other hand, have lounges with
23   antechambers.
24 SHARON: La dee da! Here, feel this towel. Did you ever feel
25   anything this creamy? *(She begins to fold it.)*
26 CARRIE: What are you doing?
27 SHARON: Taking the towel.
28 CARRIE: You're stealing the towels?
29 SHARON: Towel, singular. They'll never miss it. *(She sticks the*
30   *towel in her bag and bites a chocolate.)* Yum, strawberry.
31   *(She proceeds to put several into a baggy.)*
32 DONNA: I'm glad you had the foresight to put a couple of
33   these plastic zip-locks in your purse before we left.
34 CARRIE: You're taking the candy?
35 SHARON: Just a few. We'll need dessert, won't we? I'll just

1   move the shrimp over here and put these cheese puff
2   pastries in my cosmetic bag.
3 DONNA: Hey, let me have one of those puff things before you
4   close your purse up. Yum!
5 CARRIE: You two are too much. Well, did you at least take
6   some of those crab-stuffed mushrooms? Those are my
7   favorite hors d'oeuvres.
8 SHARON: Of course. I'm thinking of you. You going to use the
9   bathroom?
10 CARRIE: In a minute. *(She bites into another chocolate.)*
11 SHARON: Are you going to need help with that landmass of
12   fabric you have on?
13 CARRIE: *(Looking at herself in a full-length mirror, not at all*
14   *happy with the reflection)* God, would you look at this?
15   The only way my hips would look any bigger was if I were
16   wearing a bustle. Damn, it looks like I *am* wearing a
17   bustle. I hate Megan and her whole damned wedding.
18 SHARON: Why did you agree to be a part of it then?
19 CARRIE: She's one of my best friends. What could I say? Look
20   at me. If this dress were any wider I'd need a building
21   permit to wear it.
22 SHARON: You look fine. Really.
23 CARRIE: You never could lie, Sharon.
24 SHARON: Well, its one redeeming feature is that I'm not in it.
25   It is ghastly, isn't it?
26 CARRIE: And of course, everyone we ever went to high school
27   with is here. Didn't Megan make any friends at all after
28   we graduated? It's like sitting in senior square at lunch
29   five years ago. I'm a grown-up person. So, tell me, why did
30   I feel the sudden urge to start a food fight across the altar?
31 SHARON: Totally! This wedding is like some heinous little
32   reunion.
33 DONNA: To add insult to injury, did you see Ryan?
34 CARRIE: Ryan Coller? Ryan is here? *(She rushes to door and*
35   *peeks out.)* Where? I saw him during the wedding at the

1   church, but I didn't think he was invited to the reception.
2   I didn't see him.
3 DONNA: *(Joining her)* He's here, trust me. Look, over there!
4 CARRIE: Oh, fine! Well, this is sure confirmation that prayers
5   go unanswered. If they were, he'd be dead. He is evil.
6 SHARON: Still looks good, though.
7 CARRIE: So does a pirahna, but they kill without a second
8   thought.
9 SHARON: It's been five years. He's got to have changed.
10   People change.
11 CARRIE: That boy was born evil, will live evil and die evil.
12   Jeez, look at him. The way he struts around still annoys
13   me beyond any sense of endurance. Serious case of short
14   man's disease.
15 SHARON: Still has that cute little butt.
16 DONNA: *(Looking admiringly)* Yes, he does, yes, he does.
17 CARRIE: Oh my God! He's got a bald spot!
18 SHARON: Shut up! No way. *(She looks again.)* Oh! Ryan Coller
19   is losing his hair.
20 CARRIE: Ha! Who says there is no justice? I feel better already.
21 SHARON: You going to talk to him?
22 CARRIE: Why wouldn't I? I have all *my* hair!
23 SHARON: Now, now, don't be bitter.
24 CARRIE: Physician, heal thyself. I watched you at the church
25   during the wedding when Ryan walked in. You haven't
26   batted your eyes and blushed like that since the morning
27   after you made out with him for four hours up on
28   Skyline Canyon Road. It was a pretty little display of teen
29   angst revisited, I must say.
30 SHARON: Oh, please. I barely noticed he was there. Sitting
31   in the third row back, sixth from the aisle wearing
32   the tweed jacket with the dark blue shirt that matches
33   his eyes. Hardly acknowledged him. God, he is still
34   devastatingly handsome, isn't he? Even with the slight
35   hair loss.

1   DONNA: From what I hear he's doing pretty well for himself.
2   CARRIE: How so?
3   DONNA: Apparently he made some good friends at college
4   and through the alumni group he met some people who
5   got him hooked up with a really terrific job in
6   advertising.
7   CARRIE: Stanford, right? He went to Stanford.
8   SHARON: I believe he got some big scholarship or something.
9   CARRIE: He was always so arrogant. Remember how he just
10   dogged Bert, who was supposedly his best friend?
11 SHARON: It's not his fault Bert couldn't go to Stanford.
12 DONNA: And it's not like Bert made any huge effort since
13   high school to better himself. He could have gone to
14   the JC for two years and then transferred. But, no, it
15   was easier for him just to hang around town and be a
16   big nothing.
17 CARRIE: Yeah, well, that doesn't matter. Ryan turned out to
18   be some best friend. Just leaving Bert in his dust.
19 SHARON: Ryan did what he had to do to better himself.
20   *(CARRIE scoffs.)* You are not seriously telling me that you
21   would have turned down a full scholarship to Stanford
22   University to stay stuck in this podunk little town with
23   your loser best friend?
24 DONNA: Hey!
25 CARRIE: You're not a loser.
26 SHARON: I didn't mean...I mean...You know what I mean.
27 CARRIE: Yeah, I know what you mean. No, I guess I wouldn't
28   turn it down, but, jeez, he could have at least kept in
29   touch with Bert.
30 SHARON: People grow, they change. At least most of them do.
31 CARRIE: Well, that's the theory. However, some of us stay the
32   same year after stinking year.
33 SHARON: Now who's bitter?
34 CARRIE: I know, I know. I guess this wedding is a bit much
35   for me. Here I am, almost twenty-four years old and my

1   life is every bit as boring and mundane as the day I
2   graduated from high school. Where the hell did the last
3   five years go? How can I still be working at the
4   SuperCenter Market? Still?!
5 DONNA: You're assistant manager. That's pretty good.
6 CARRIE: Great. So is this my future? I don't remember my
7   high school dreams including the words, "Clean up on
8   aisle seven." And, hell, I can't remember the last time I
9   had a date with someone who even remotely looked like
10   he could turn into a part of my future.
11 SHARON: You'll find someone. *(CARRIE looks at her*
12   *doubtfully.)* It's the truth. Megan married someone
13   terrific. Megan! She still wears her hair in those stupid
14   little poofs on top and the flips at the side. If she can find
15   a man like Charlie, there's hope for even the most
16   disfigured and deformed.
17 DONNA: Well, thanks so much.
18 CARRIE: Yeah, Sharon. By all means, keep a good thought.
19 SHARON: You know that came out totally wrong.
20 CARRIE: I know.
21 SHARON: I don't know why you are so down.
22 CARRIE: Look at us, Sharon. Here's our lives in a nutshell: No
23   college educations, dead-end jobs, and our lives alone.
24 SHARON: You *do* have Bert, you know.
25 CARRIE: Hello, consolation prize.
26 SHARON: He's good to you.
27 DONNA: He's a loser.
28 CARRIE: Yes, he's good to me. But you're right, he's a loser.
29   There's no future there.
30 DONNA: He's still stuck in the land of "woulda, coulda,
31   shoulda." He couldn't afford Stanford, and he's made it
32   his crutch as to why the rest of his life hasn't come
33   together. Waa, waa, waa.
34 CARRIE: He's a good guy. He's only ever going to be a nice
35   interim kind of guy, but he certainly isn't husband material.

1   SHARON: Then stop seeing him.

2   CARRIE: I can't do that. He'd be so hurt. So here I am, stuck.

3   DONNA: I know what you mean. It's like one dead end after
4   another around here.

5   SHARON: I don't feel that way. I'm pretty happy with myself
6   right now. I am only twenty-three years old. That's
7   young. would you seriously want to get married now,
8   like Megan?

9   CARRIE: If I could find a guy like Charlie? In a heartbeat.

10 SHARON: You're really ready to give up the single life? Not
11   me! I want to do things and try things and go places that
12   if I were married I just couldn't. I want to travel. I want
13   to take some classes at the college. Maybe I will get a
14   degree in something. The point is, I can do all that if and
15   when I want, because there is no one I have to think
16   about except myself. Just me. It's such a feeling of
17   freedom.

18 CARRIE: You can do all that stuff with a husband.

19 SHARON: Nah, I don't think so. Because when you're married
20   there's all kinds of other things to think about.
21   Mortgages, bills, car payments. Kids!

22 CARRIE: A mortgage means a home. Bills and car payments
23   are something you share with someone. And kids – kids
24   mean you have a future. Kids give you a really good
25   reason not to smoke.

26 SHARON: Life gives you a good reason, Care. Life does.

27 DONNA: I know what you mean, Sharon. Since I've gone back
28   to school, you know, I don't feel as out of control of things
29   as I used to. That tumbleweed thing.

30 CARRIE: Tumbleweed?

31 DONNA: Have you ever seen a tumbleweed? It's this big ugly
32   thing just being pushed everywhere by a wind that
33   doesn't give a damn about what's blowing through it's
34   path. That's how my life was, but not anymore. I'm not
35   the tumbleweed, I'm the wind.

1   CARRIE: Let's all sing a round of *Kumbayah*.

2   DONNA: Make remarks, that's fine. But I'm in control of what
3   I'm doing with my life; I'm not waiting for things to
4   happen.

5   SHARON: Exactly! You can't always be looking outside
6   yourself for something to *make* you happy. Life makes
7   you happy, the way you choose to live it.

8   CARRIE: I don't know. You're both right. I look at Megan,
9   even with those little poofs on top of her head; she
10   looked so beautiful. And Charlie looked so happy. Did
11   you see them? There is such a future there. I want
12   something like that.

13   SHARON: It will come.

14   CARRIE: Yeah? So what do I do until then?

15   SHARON: Well, you certainly don't sit around feeling sorry
16   for yourself. Good grief, Carrie. Why are you acting
17   like this?

18   CARRIE: Maybe because I *am* beginning to realize that my
19   future is in my hands. You know what you said about
20   breaking up with Bert? That's what I've been thinking
21   about for quite a while. I just don't know how to do that
22   without really hurting him.

23   DONNA: It will be just one more little failure for him in a long
24   line of little failures. He's going nowhere fast and he's
25   taking you with him.

26   CARRIE: I don't want to hurt him, though.

27   SHARON: Isn't it hurting him more to stay with him just
28   because he's better than nothing?

29   CARRIE: Put that way, I can see what you mean.

30   SHARON: Your problem is that you're comfortable. You stay
31   in the same job that you hate, you stay with the same guy
32   you don't love. It's easier to stay and be safe and unhappy
33   than to risk it all to go for much more. Personally, I'll
34   take the risk. I'll be damned if at our ten-year high school
35   reunion I show up having accomplished nothing more

1 than what I have now. Do you want to show up with Bert
2 on your arm, a snotty kid on your hip and your
3 SuperCenter Market nameplate on your lapel?
4 CARRIE: On my God, no!
5 SHARON: Then do something about it. Megan's wedding day
6 should be our anniversary date for the three of us for the
7 rest of our lives. We should mark this day down and
8 make sure that by the same time next year we've
9 accomplished something more than we have today. And
10 every year it should get better and better.
11 CARRIE: Donna, how did you get the courage to go back to
12 school at twenty-four? By the time you're done you'll be
13 almost thirty.
14 DONNA: I figure I'm going to be thirty anyway, so what the
15 hell. I might as well be thirty with a degree that will
16 make the next fifty years of my life something worth
17 living.
18 CARRIE: You're right. It's time for a change. A big change. OK.
19 As soon as this thing is over I am going to strip out of this
20 burden of a dress and make a list of things I want to do.
21 Scratch that. These are things I *need* to do. And the first
22 will be to break up with Bert. God, that's going to be
23 hard. He is such a sweet guy.
24 DONNA: A sweet guy with no future.
25 CARRIE: I haven't been without Bert for three years. Whew, I
26 will be alone. Alone.
27 SHARON: You won't be alone. You'll have your dreams and
28 your future and who knows what else that's out there.
29 CARRIE: Scary stuff.
30 DONNA: The unknown usually is. But it's better than stocking
31 the shelves in the frozen food department.
32 SHARON: And the unknown own can be exciting, huh?
33 CARRIE: Yeah, it can be. In a scary way. Maybe I will just
34 smoke this one last cig as a symbol of my old life being
35 burned away. *(SHARON looks at her dubiously.)* No, huh?

1   OK, new attitude, fresh start.
2   SHARON: And, hey, no matter what, we'll always have each
3   other's support.
4   CARRIE: Promise?
5   SHARON: Promise! *(She picks up a chocolate and holds it up in*
6   *a toast.)* To the future.
7   DONNA: *(Joining her with a chocolate)* To the unknown.
8   CARRIE: *(Picking up her own chocolate and toasting with it)* To
9   what's ahead....no matter how scary.
10
11
12
13
14
15
16
17
18
19
20
21
22
23
24
25
26
27
28
29
30
31
32
33
34
35

Old Habits

(Scene for three men and two women)

1   *(Outside at the wedding reception for Megan and Charlie.*
2   *GEORGE, RON and TODD enter excitedly. KATE and*
3   *CAROLYN stand off to one side before joining them.)*
4   **GEORGE:** *(Entering excitedly, followed by RON and TODD)* Did
5   you see that crowd? They loved us! Loved us! Everyone
6   was dancing, everyone was into it. We were awesome!
7   **TODD:** I've been telling you, this band is just too good to be
8   playing weddings and bar mitzvahs. You should be
9   touring. You should be promoted. You need a manager.
10   Someone with enthusiasm and energy. And I am the
11   man to do it.
12   **KATE:** *(Entering with CAROLYN)* Uh-oh, looks like our men
13   are up to something.
14   **CAROLYN:** With Todd right in the middle of it all. God, he's
15   a pain.
16   **KATE:** He's all right.
17   **CAROLYN:** I knew they shouldn't have played here tonight.
18   **KATE:** They were great, though. The crowd loved them.
19   **CAROLYN:** The audience loved everything they played. And
20   why wouldn't they? Everyone at this wedding has known
21   everyone else since grammar school. It's not like it's a
22   tough crowd.
23   **GEORGE:** Carolyn, honey, come over here and give me a big
24   sloppy kiss. I'm telling you guys, we are this close to
25   making it and I mean making it big time. *(The girls join*
26   *the guys.)*
27   **TODD:** I believe in you. Your music is great! The sounds, the
28   rhythms, the harmonies. You are hot. Hot! Ron, do you
29   understand what we are saying?
30   **RON:** Yeah, hot, big time. I get it. But the fact remains, we are
31   a small-time band...
32   **TODD:** Just waiting to hit it big.
33   **GEORGE:** You know we are, man. Big!
34   **RON:** I know you want to believe it, but Bobby and Stan just
35   don't have time for this. And to be honest, neither do I.

1   (*He puts his arm around KATE.*)
2   TODD: Time? George, the man is talking about time. Time,
3   my young friend, is on our side. We're young, we're free,
4   you're talented and I'm smart. Put it all together and it
5   stinks to high heaven of success.
6   KATE: It stinks to high heaven of something.
7   RON: You seem to forget something. I'm not free. I'm getting
8   married, I'm working on my teaching credential. Stan is
9   serious about his ministry work. And you both know
10   Bobby isn't interested in being anything but a garage band.
11   TODD; So we lose him. Anyone can play bass. But we need
12   your keyboards and Stan's horns. And do you know a
13   better singer than George? You do not. Let me handle
14   everything...
15   CAROLYN: What do you mean handle everything?
16   GEORGE: Todd was telling me that he could get us some real
17   leads to some big jobs, maybe even recording.
18   CAROLYN: Todd was telling you this?
19   KATE: Gee, Todd, another big scheme?
20   TODD: This is the big one, Kate, the big one. Trust me.
21   RON: You keep saying we can make it. Thousands of guys in
22   bands all over the country are saying the same thing.
23   GEORGE: Yeah? Well, they don't have me, now do they? I
24   didn't think so.
25   RON: I don't know. Kate, what do you think?
26   KATE: I think you need to do what you need to do. And if
27   doing this rock star thing is it, with Todd in charge, well,
28   that's up to you. I told you from the start that I wouldn't
29   interfere with your music. (*Looking pointedly at TODD*)
30   No matter what lame brain came up with the idea.
31   TODD: See? She's one hundred percent behind you.
32   CAROLYN: I don't know.
33   GEORGE: What do you mean, "You don't know"?
34   CAROLYN: Sweetie, it's the same thing all over again. You get
35   all pumped about your music and everything else falls

1   apart. It lasts for a couple months then you're back doing

2   what you usually do...

3   GEORGE: Which is?

4   CAROLYN: Who knows. Floating? Not facing your responsibil-

5   ities and getting depressed because your life is going

6   nowhere. Old habits with you.

7   TODD: That was before, Carolyn. Now he's serious.

8   CAROLYN: He's always serious. For about two months, then

9   he's back to being George.

10   GEORGE: Well, it's nice to know that the woman in my life is

11   going to be there to cheer me on.

12   KATE: She has a point, you know.

13   RON: Katie, honey, this isn't our argument.

14   KATE: You're right. Sorry, none of my business.

15   GEORGE: No, I think I'd like to hear what you have to say.

16   Please, let's do what we usually do and let the women

17   rain on our parade.

18   CAROLYN: That's a little unfair.

19   GEORGE: Is it? I don't think so. Look at you. Every time I

20   want to really focus on my music, you have to find some

21   way of bringing me down.

22   KATE: Can you blame her? You're planning on putting Todd

23   in charge of managing the band? Now, that's a *good*

24   idea. Please, why not give him access to your credit cards,

25   as well?

26   TODD: *(Just as sarcastic back to her)* That's a really nice

27   attitude to have towards me. Thank you so much.

28   CAROLYN: Well, jeez, Todd, it isn't like this is the first time

29   you've gotten some wild hair about some scheme to

30   make it big.

31   RON: I really think just the guys should discuss this.

32   KATE: Just the *guys* should discuss this? *Pardon.*

33   RON: Kate, it's my band. You said that you wouldn't interfere

34   with my music.

35   KATE: I'm not interfering. I'm offering an observation.

1 RON: Well, for the time being, why don't you keep your
2   observations to yourself?
3 KATE: To myself? If this is what you think marriage is all
4   about, where we don't discuss plans that will determine
5   the future for both of us, perhaps we should rethink the
6   whole idea.
7 RON: You're overreacting.
8 KATE: Like hell I am.
9 CAROLYN: I think we're losing sight of the major point here.
10 TODD: Hey! We were talking about the band, not your lives.
11 KATE: Apparently one excludes the other.
12 GEORGE: I don't get it. Two minutes ago everything was
13   awesome. Now everyone is upset with everyone else.
14 CAROLYN: No one is upset.
15 GEORGE: I am!
16 TODD: Just listen to me! This time it will all be different. I
17   met this guy who's got a friend who knows the keyboard
18   player for Springsteen! He said he could arrange to have
19   that demo tape we made sent to that guy and get it
20   listened to!
21 KATE: Well! What are we waiting for? Grab the cat, pack a bag
22   and let's all head for Hollywood right now!
23 GEORGE: Ha ha. Funny.
24 RON: Kate, the least you could do is hear him out.
25 CAROLYN: And how will all this meeting and arranging and
26   listening happen?
27 TODD: Well, I haven't got that part worked out yet...
28 CAROLYN: Well, there's a real surprise.
29 GEORGE: Carolyn, why are you being so nasty about this?
30 CAROLYN: You ask why? You really don't know?
31 TODD: If he knew, he wouldn't ask.
32 CAROLYN: OK, fine, I'll tell you. And Todd, you should recall
33   this better than anyone. Remember two years ago when
34   this band first started getting good? You guys were
35   playing some of the local clubs and stuff. And all those

1   girls were hanging all over you. That didn't bother me.

2   You know what bothered me? The fact that you loved it.

3   And you loved it right in front of me. And you expected

4   me to just sit back like some retro woman from the

5   fifties, keep my mouth shut and let you have your fun.

6   GEORGE: I said I was sorry.

7   CAROLYN: Yeah, after the band fell apart and you guys quit

8   playing and there were no more babes hanging around.

9   Then, you were sorry and then you wanted me.

10   GEORGE: It was a mistake, OK? Can't someone make a mistake?

11   KATE: Mistake? George, come on. Personally, I can't believe

12   she took you back. If Ron ever did that, *bam!* Over!

13   RON: Here we go. It's the same argument every time, just in a

14   different edition. If it's not the women, it's the time, if it's

15   not the time, it's something else. Todd, I told you this

16   wouldn't work.

17   GEORGE: Hey, if you're talking about last night, that wasn't

18   my fault.

19   RON: You *knew* we had a rehearsal scheduled. Playing for

20   Megan and Charlie's wedding and reception wasn't just a

21   paying job. It was a commitment that I took seriously

22   because it was for people we all really care about.

23   GEORGE: I couldn't help that.

24   RON: You were two hours late for practice, man. Two hours.

25   GEORGE: It wasn't my fault. They scheduled me to work the

26   dinner shift. I had to work.

27   CAROLYN: Well, at least you didn't drop that ball.

28   KATE: Wait a minute. Ron, you mean our whole evening was

29   screwed up, we couldn't go out with my family because

30   George was late for practice? That's why? I thought you

31   guys had some changes in music or something. Dammit,

32   George, you screw up everyone else's schedule just so you

33   won't be inconvenienced.

34   GEORGE: It wasn't my fault.

35   KATE: Nothing ever is, is it?

1   CAROLYN: Hey! He had to work. Todd, you remember
2   working, don't you?
3   TODD: I have a job.
4   CAROLYN: Dressing in a giant Twinkie costume and handing
5   out samples in the SuperCenter Market is not the kind of
6   ladder climbing position I'd be bragging about.
7   RON: At least he was at practice and on time.
8   TODD: And I'm not even in the band.
9   GEORGE: So what did you want me to do? Quit my job?
10   RON: You don't have to quit.
11   CAROLYN: For God's sake, no, don't quit. This is the longest
12   you've ever had a job.
13   TODD: Well, you might have to quit if this guy who's going to
14   listen to the band likes what he hears.
15   CAROLYN: Why would he have to quit.
16   GEORGE: I'd have to focus, really focus on what I was doing
17   with my music. We all would.
18   KATE: All? *(She looks at RON.)* All? Is that what you'd do, too?
19   RON: I haven't given it much thought.
20   TODD: Much thought? That's all we've talked about for the last
21   two months. Why do you think I humiliate myself by
22   dressing up in that ridiculous outfit? Do you think I enjoy
23   looking like a giant dessert? Do you think it's fun having
24   some fool grab you by the large plastic nose and squeezing
25   sample pieces of Twinkie on your fluorescent green vest
26   while he demands you dance for the gathering crowds?
27   GEORGE: I did it once.
28   TODD: My point is, I have a job that is flexible so I can work
29   on this band and it's future. I seem to care more than the
30   rest of you.
31   KATE: Todd, you're doing it again.
32   TODD: Doing what?
33   KATE: Living off of other people's dreams. The guys in the
34   band have talent, they have something to offer. You are just
35   looking to latch on to that and use it to your advantage.

1   RON: That's a little rough, Kate.
2   CAROLYN: Maybe it is, Ron, but she's speaking facts. Todd,
3   you've done the same thing ever since high school. You
4   had so much to offer, so much going for you and you
5   didn't do a damn thing with it.
6   RON: Come on, give the guy a little credit. He's getting us to
7   Springsteen.
8   KATE: He's getting you to a friend of a friend of Springsteen's
9   keyboard player. Big whoop.
10 GEORGE: I don't care what anyone else says. I'm going for it.
11 RON: You say that now. But what happens when we have
12   practice and you get called into work again?
13 GEORGE: I won't go. This could be our big break.
14 CAROLYN: Oh, fine. That's just great. Face it, George, you're
15   going to float from one dead-end job to another, always
16   hoping that the big break is around the corner.
17   And while you're waiting for that big break, everyone
18   else is getting on with their lives and making something
19   out of them.
20 GEORGE: If we do this, the whole band does it.
21 TODD: It's got to be a total commitment.
22 CAROLYN: You really think that Stan and Ron and Bobby are
23   going to give up futures so they can be back-up players to
24   your lead singing? Not in this lifetime.
25 TODD: They won't be back-up players. It's a band. A group, a
26   family of artists. It's worth any sacrifice.
27 RON: Hold on there, guys. I'm not willing to make the sacrifice
28   of a future. I've got my intern teaching year coming up in
29   September. That involves grading papers, doing lesson
30   plans, the whole teaching shot. And I don't get paid for it.
31   So, not only will I be doing that, I have to work.
32 KATE: We're getting married in a year, don't forget. We have
33   to save for that.
34 RON: That's right.
35 GEORGE: Save for what? How much does it cost to get married?

1   KATE: Look at Megan and Charlie's wedding. Do you think all
2   this was free?
3   TODD: Forget the big wedding. Elope. Ron, you need to get
4   your priorities straight.
5   CAROLYN: Maybe he has them straight already.
6   GEORGE: Dammit, Ron, why are you throwing away this chance?
7   RON: I'm not throwing anything away. There's nothing there
8   to throw. Face it, we're a garage band and that's all we are
9   ever going to be. At least this group. I'm not giving up a
10   sure and safe future for some wild dream.
11 GEORGE: I can' believe you! *(To KATE)* This is all because of
12   you. He wouldn't be doing this if you weren't here
13   screwing everything up.
14 KATE: I didn't tell him what to do. I never have. And I said I
15   would support him no matter what. But he's got to
16   support me, too.
17 TODD: Oh, so he gives up his dreams so you can live the life
18   of some stay-at-home housewife?
19 RON: That's not what it is at all. It's two people who love each
20   other and have a life and future planned together. It's
21   about responsibilities to each other and the family that
22   we want.
23 GEORGE: What about responsibilities to yourself?
24 RON: That future *is* me. It's both of us. I look at Kate and see
25   my whole life in front of me. I'm not going to throw that
26   away for an idea that maybe someone will hear us and
27   think we have promise. I have promise now, with Kate.
28 KATE: I really do love you, you know that?
29 GEORGE: Brother.
30 TODD: I'm dying here! I'm dying!
31 CAROLYN: You are so lucky.
32 GEORGE: Lucky? He's tied down, shackled, hamstrung.
33 CAROLYN: Is that how you see it? Then I feel sorry for you, I
34   really do. They've got a life that they are planning
35   together. Together, George. One that includes both of

1   them. What do we have? Me, waiting around to see if
2   you're going to get fired from yet another minimum wage
3   job, and you trying to be the next Bon Jovi. It could take
4   years and years and then never happen. And where do I
5   end up?
6 GEORGE: You're a part of that. Why is my plan so less
7   significant than Ron's? What makes his better? Because
8   it's teaching, it's traditional, it's socially acceptable?
9 TODD: You know that's what it is. If you were going to spend
10   the same amount of time trying to be a doctor, she'd be
11   all for it. But because it's music, it's a silly dream.
12 CAROLYN: That's not it at all. If you'd just stick with
13   something for longer than it takes a two-year-old to get
14   bored, then maybe I could support you. But you don't.
15   You talk big, you make plans, and then you get tired of
16   the work it takes to make it happen and you're off doing
17   something else.
18 RON: You know she's right. Hell, George, it's getting to where
19   we don't know if you are going to show up for practice
20   from one day to the next.
21 GEORGE: You know I'll be there.
22 RON: We don't *know*. Look, you were two hours late last night.
23 GEORGE: It couldn't be helped. I had to work.
24 RON: So do the rest of us, but we managed.
25 KATE: You aren't the only one who makes sacrifices so this
26   band can stay working, you know. Not only Ron, but Stan
27   and Bobby give up things. So do Carolyn and I. And Todd,
28   so does Jennifer.
29 TODD: Jennifer has nothing to do with this.
30 KATE: You know, you think she's always going to be there,
31   waiting around for your next scheme to unfold. She's got
32   a future to think of, too.
33 TODD: Jennifer is perfectly happy with the way our life is.
34 CAROLYN: Perhaps you should check that out. Because I, for
35   one, have about had it. George, you need to grow up. Face

1   the fact that you are never going to be a rock star the way
2   you're going now...
3 GEORGE: You have no faith in my talents. No one does – not
4   my sister, not the guys in the band, not even you.
5 CAROLYN: I have every faith in your talent. It's your
6   dedication that I question.
7 RON: So do we.
8 GEORGE: To hell with you then. To hell with the band, to hell
9   with you, Carolyn.
10 TODD: What do you mean to hell with the band?
11 GEORGE: You want to manage something? Manage me.
12 TODD: But the band...the tape...
13 GEORGE: Hey, who's singing lead vocals? Me! Who carries
14   that band? Me! Who created that sound? Me! Just tell that
15   guy that you're managing a solo artist.
16 TODD: Are you serious?
17 GEORGE: Damn right I am. You guys think I'm a loser? You
18   think Todd is a loser? Watch us. In one year, I guarantee
19   you, we will be making our first record. *(Looking at RON)*
20   With or without you.
21 RON: You do what you have to do.
22 CAROLYN: What about me? What about us?
23 GEORGE: You're either with me or against me. Make up
24   your mind.
25 KATE: That's not fair to her, George.
26 GEORGE: She's either along for the ride or she gets off the
27   roller coaster.
28 CAROLYN: Then I guess I get off. I've been through this kind
29   of quick-start enthusiasm with you one too many times. I
30   can't go through it again.
31 GEORGE: You better think it over.
32 CAROLYN: There's nothing to think over. It's not that I don't
33   believe you can do it, that you have the talent to make it. I
34   just don't think you want to put in the work it would take.
35 TODD: I think he does.

239

1   GEORGE: I know I do. And I will. Watch me. Come on, Todd,
2   we have some serious planning to do.
3   TODD: Right behind you. Hey, if you see Jennifer, tell her I'll
4   catch up with her later. *(They exit.)*
5   RON: Well, so much for our band.
6   KATE: You OK?
7   RON: Yeah, I knew it would have to end sooner or later. I just
8   thought it would be later.
9   KATE: Carolyn?
10   CAROLYN: I'm fine. I'm like Ron, I knew it would end. George
11   doesn't want a partner, he wants a fan club. I can't be
12   blind to his faults. And I can't stick around catching him
13   every time he falls.
14   KATE: You want to leave?
15   CAROLYN: No. I think I'll go in and toast the happy
16   newlyweds and figure out what I'm going to do with the
17   rest of my life. *(She exits.)*
18   KATE: Ron, are you OK with this? You don't feel like I'm
19   pressuring you to make a decision you don't want to
20   make, do you?
21   RON: No. I really don't. I wish George the best of luck. If he
22   makes it, great. But I don't have that desire. I want to
23   teach, I want to marry you and I want kids. It's a small
24   dream to him, but it's a perfect dream for me.
25   KATE: I love you so much.
26   RON: You want to go back in?
27   KATE: No, let's take a walk and we'll talk about our life. *Our*
28   life. *(They exit.)*
29
30
31
32
33
34
35

ABOUT THE AUTHOR

Mary Krell-Oishi has been teaching since 1976 and began her high school theatre teaching at Sunny Hills High School in Fullerton, California, in 1984. She recently completed her Masters in Theatre Education at California State University, Fullerton and has absolutely no plans whatsoever to pursue a higher degree. One is enough, thank you very much.

Her primary career joy has been and remains teaching high school theatre and interacting with young, fresh talent. Mrs. Krell-Oishi takes great pride in the fact that she was named as Playwright of the Year by the California State Thespians at their conference in 1995. Her plans are to continue working with high school drama students and to focus her writing for them.

Still living in Yorba Linda, California, Mary Krell-Oishi devotes her time away from school to her husband, Harris, her soon-to-be-graduating-from-high-school son, Rick, and her writing.

NOTES

NOTES

ORDER FORM

MERIWETHER PUBLISHING LTD.
P.O. BOX 7710
COLORADO SPRINGS, CO 80933
TELEPHONE: (719) 594-4422

Please send me the following books:

Perspectives #TT-B206 $12.95
by Mary Krell-Oishi
Relevant scenes for teens

More Scenes That Happen #TT-B112 $12.95
by Mary Krell-Oishi
More real-life snapshots of teenage lives

Scenes That Happen #TT-B156 $12.95
by Mary Krell-Oishi
Dramatized snapshots of high school life

Winning Monologs for Young Actors #TT-B127 $14.95
by Peg Kehret
Honest-to-life monologs for young actors

Encore! More Winning Monologs for $12.95
Young Actors #TT-B144
by Peg Kehret
More honest-to-life monologs for young actors

Acting Natural #TT-B133 $12.95
by Peg Kehret
Honest-to-life monologs, dialogs and playlets for teens

Theatre Games for Young Performers $12.95
#TT-B188
by Maria C. Novelly
Improvisations and exercises for developing acting skills

**These and other fine Meriwether Publishing books are available at
your local bookstore or direct from the publisher. Use the handy
order form on this page.**

NAME: _____

ORGANIZATION NAME: _____

ADDRESS: _____

CITY: _____ STATE: _____

ZIP: _____ PHONE: _____

□ **Check Enclosed**
□ **Visa or MasterCard #** _____

                                            Expiration
Signature: _____ *Date:* _____
          (required for Visa/MasterCard orders)

COLORADO RESIDENTS: Please add 3% sales tax.
SHIPPING: Include $2.75 for the first book and 50¢ for each additional book ordered.

□ *Please send me a copy of your complete catalog of books and plays.*

ORDER FORM

MERIWETHER PUBLISHING LTD.
P.O. BOX 7710
COLORADO SPRINGS, CO 80933
TELEPHONE: (719) 594-4422

Please send me the following books:

_____ **Playing Scenes From Classic Literature** $14.95
#TT-B201
edited by **Joellen K. Bland**
Short dramatizations from world literature

_____ **Multicultural Theatre #TT-B205** $14.95
edited by **Roger Ellis**
Scenes and monologs by multicultural writers

_____ **Playing Contemporary Scenes #TT-B100** $14.95
edited by **Gerald Lee Ratliff**
Thirty-one famous scenes and how to play them

_____ **The Scenebook for Actors #TT-B177** $14.95
by **Dr. Norman A. Bert**
Collection of great monologs and dialogs for auditions

_____ **One-Act Plays for Acting Students #TT-B139** $14.95
by **Dr. Norman A. Bert**
An anthology of complete one-act plays

_____ **Theatre Alive! #TT-B178** $24.95
by **Dr. Norman A. Bert**
An introductory anthology of world drama

_____ **Playing Scenes — A Sourcebook for** $14.95
Performers #TT-B109
by **Gerald Lee Ratliff**
How to play great scenes from modern and classical theatre

These and other fine Meriwether Publishing books are available at
your local bookstore or direct from the publisher. Use the handy
order form on this page.

NAME: _____

ORGANIZATION NAME: _____

ADDRESS: _____

CITY: _____ STATE: _____

ZIP: _____ PHONE: _____

❑ **Check Enclosed**
❑ **Visa or MasterCard #** _____

                                                  Expiration
Signature: _____ *Date:* _____
        (required for Visa/MasterCard orders)

COLORADO RESIDENTS: Please add 3% sales tax.
SHIPPING: Include $2.75 for the first book and 50¢ for each additional book ordered.

❑ *Please send me a copy of your complete catalog of books and plays.*